The World's Famous Orations

VOL. V

GREAT BRITAIN—III

1865—1906

THE WORLD'S FAMOUS ORATIONS

WILLIAM JENNINGS BRYAN
EDITOR-IN-CHIEF

FRANCIS W. HALSEY
ASSOCIATE EDITOR

IN TEN VOLUMES

Vol. V
GREAT BRITAIN—III

FUNK and WAGNALLS COMPANY
New York and London

CONTENTS

Vol. V—Great Britain—III (1865—1906)

CONTENTS

Page

VOL. V

GREAT BRITAIN—III

1865—1906

MACDONALD

ON CANADIAN CONFEDERATION [1]
(1865)

Born in 1815, died in 1891; Receiver-General in Canada in 1847; Attorney-General in 1854; Prime Minister in 1857, and again in 1868 and 1878· one of the British Commissioners who signed the Treaty of Washington; leader in work of effecting Canadian confederation.

I HAVE had the honor of being charged, on behalf of the government, to submit a scheme for the confederation of all the British North American Provinces—a scheme which has been received, I am glad to say, with general if not universal approbation in Canada. This subject is not a new one. For years it has more or less attracted the attention of every statesman and politician in these provinces, and has been looked upon by many far-seeing politicians as being eventually the means of deciding and settling very many of the vexed questions which have retarded the prosperity of the Colonies as a whole, and particularly the prosperity of Canada.

The subject, however, tho looked upon with

[1] Delivered in the Parliament of Canada in February, 1865, Macdonald (not yet Sir John) being then attorney-general. Two years later, when the Union was effected, he became prime minister. Abridged.

favor by the country, and tho there were no distinct expressions of opposition to it from any party, did not begin to assume its present proportions until the last session. Then men of all parties and all shades of politics became alarmed at the aspect of affairs. They found that such was the opposition between the two sections of the Province, such was the danger of impending anarchy in consequence of the irreconcilable differences of opinion with respect to representation by population between Upper and Lower Canada, that unless some solution of the difficulty was arrived at we would suffer under a succession of weak governments—weak in numerical support, weak in force, and weak in power of doing good.

In the proposed constitution all matters of general interest are to be dealt with by the general legislature; while the local legislatures will deal with matters of local interest which do not affect the confederation as a whole, but are of the greatest importance to their particular sections. By such a division of labor the sittings of the general legislature would not be so protracted as even those of Canada alone. And so with the local legislatures: their attention being confined to subjects pertaining to their own sections, their sessions would be shorter and less expensive.

Then, when we consider the enormous saving that will be effected in the administration of affairs by one general government; when we re-

flect that each of the five Colonies has a government of its own with a complete establishment of
public departments and all the machinery required for the transaction of the business of the
country; that each has a separate executive, judi-
cial, and militia system; that each Province has
a separate ministry, including a minister of
militia, with a complete adjutant-general's department; that each has a finance minister, with
a full customs and excise staff; that each Colony
has as large and complete and administrative organization with as many executive officers as the
general government will have—we can well
understand the enormous saving that will result
from a union of all the Colonies, from their
having but one head and one central system.
We in Canada already know something of the
advantages and disadvantages of a federal union.

The whole scheme of confederation as pro-
pounded by the conference as agreed to and
sanctioned by the Canadian government, and
as now presented for the consideration of the
people and the legislature, bears upon its face
the marks of compromise. Of necessity there
must have been a great deal of mutual discussion. When we think of the representatives
of five Colonies, all supposed to have different
interests, meeting together, charged with the
duty of protecting those interests and of press-
ing the views of their own localities and sections,
it must be admitted that had we not met in a
spirit of conciliation and with an anxious desire

to promote this union; if we had not been impressed with the idea contained in the words of the resolution,—"that the best interests and present and future prosperity of British North America would be promoted by a federal union under the Crown of Great Britain,"—all our efforts might have proved to be of no avail. If we had not felt that, after coming to this conclusion, we were bound to set aside our private opinions on matters of detail; if we had not felt ourselves bound to look at what was practicable—not obstinately rejecting the opinions of others nor adhering to our own; if we had not met, I say, in a spirit of conciliation, and with an anxious, overruling desire to form one people under one government, we never would have succeeded.

With these views we press the question on this House and the country. I say to this House, if you do not believe that the union of the Colonies is for the advantage of the country, that the joining of these five peoples into one nation under one sovereign is for the benefit of all, then reject the scheme. Reject if you do not believe it to be for the present advantage and future prosperity of yourselves and your children. But if, after a calm and full consideration of this scheme, it is believed, as a whole, to be for the advantage of this Province—if the House and country believe this union to be one which will ensure for us British laws, British connection, and British freedom, and increase and develop the social, political, and material prosperity of the country—then I implore this House and the country to lay aside all prejudices and accept the scheme which we offer. I ask this House to meet the question in the same spirit in which the delegates met it. I ask each member of this House to lay aside his own opinions as to particular details and to accept the scheme as to a whole, if he think it beneficial as a whole.

As I stated in the preliminary discussion, we must consider this scheme in the light of a treaty. By the happy coincidence of circumstances, just when an administration had been formed in Canada for the purpose of attempting a solution of the difficulties under which we labored, at the same time the Lower Provinces, actuated by a similar feeling, appointed a conference with a view to a union among themselves, without being cognizant of the position the government was taking in Canada. If it had not been for this fortunate coincidence of events, never, perhaps, for a long series of years would we have been able to bring this scheme to a practical conclusion. But we did succeed. We made the arrangement, agreed upon the scheme, and the deputations from the several governments represented at the Conference went back pledged to lay it before their governments, and to ask the legislatures and people of their respective Provinces to assent to it. I trust the scheme will be assented to as a whole. I am sure this

House will not seek to alter it in its unimportant details; and if altered in any important provisions the result must be that the whole will be set aside and we must begin *de novo*. If any important changes are made, every one of the Colonies will feel itself absolved from the implied obligation to deal with it as a treaty, each Province will feel itself at liberty to amend it *ad libitum* so as to suit its own views and interests; in fact the whole of our labors will have been for naught, and we will have to renew our negotiations with all the colonies for the purpose of establishing some new scheme.

I hope the House will not adopt any such course as will postpone, perhaps for ever, or at all events for a long period, all chances of union. All the statesmen and public men who have written or spoken on the subject admit the advantages of a union if it were practicable; and now, when it is proved to be practicable, if we do not embrace this opportunity, the present favorable time will pass away, and we may never have it again. Because, just so surely as this scheme is defeated, will be revived the original proposition for a union of the Maritime Provinces irrespective of Canada; they will not remain as they are now, powerless, scattered, helpless communities; they will form themselves into a power which, tho not so strong as if united with Canada, will nevertheless be a powerful and considerable community, and it will be then too late for us to attempt to strengthen ourselves by this scheme, which, in the words of the resolution, "is for the best interests and present and future prosperity of British North America."

If we are not blind to our present position we must see the hazardous situation in which all the great interests of Canada stand in respect to the United States. I am no alarmist, I do not believe in the prospect of immediate war. I believe that the common sense of the two nations will prevent a war; still we can not trust to probabilities. The government and legislature would be wanting in their duty to the people if they ran any risk. We know that the United States at this moment are engaged in a war of enormous dimensions: that the occasion of a war with Great Britain has again and again arisen and may at any time in the future again arise. We can not foresee what may be the result; we can not say but that the two nations may drift into a war as other nations have done before. It would then be too late, when war had commenced, to think of measures for strengthening ourselves or to begin negotiations for a union with the sister Provinces.

At this moment, in consequence of the ill feeling which has arisen between England and the United States—a feeling of which Canada was not the cause—in consequence of the irritation which now exists owing to the unhappy state of affairs on this continent, the reciprocity treaty, it seems probable, is about to be brought to an end; our trade is hampered by the passport system, and at any moment we may be deprived of permission to carry our goods through United States channels; the bonded goods system may be done away with, and the winter trade through the United States put an end to. Our merchants may be obliged to return to the old system of bringing in during the summer months the supplies for the whole year. Ourselves already threatened, our trade interrupted, our intercourse, political and commercial, destroyed, if we do not take warning now when we have the opportunity, and, while one avenue is threatened to be closed, open another by taking advantage of the present arrangement and the desire of the Lower Provinces to draw closer the alliance between us, we may suffer commercial and political disadvantages it may take long for us to overcome.

It is the fashion now to enlarge on the defects of the Constitution of the United States, but I am not one of those who look upon it as a failure. I think and believe that it is one of the most skilful works which human intelligence ever created; is one of the most perfect organizations that ever governed a free people. To say that it has some defects is but to say that it is not the work of omniscience, but of human intellects. We are happily situated in having had the opportunity of watching its operation, seeing its working from its infancy till now. It was in the main formed on the model of the

Constitution of Great Britain, adapted to the circumstances of a new country, and was perhaps the only practicable system that could have been adopted under the circumstances existing at the time of its formation. We can now take advantage of the experience of the last seventy-eight years during which that Constitution has existed, and I am strongly in the belief that we have in a great measure avoided in this system which we propose for the adoption of the people of Canada the defects which time and events have shown to exist in the American Constitution.

In the first place, by a resolution which meets with the universal approval of the people of this country, we have provided that for all time to come, so far as we can legislate for the future, we shall have as the head of the executive power the sovereign of Great Britain. No one can look into futurity and say what will be the destiny of this country. Changes come over nations and peoples in the course of ages. But so far as we can legislate we provide that for all time to come the sovereign of Great Britain shall be the sovereign of British North America. By adhering to the monarchical principle we avoid one defect inherent in the Constitution of the United States. By the election of the president by a majority and for a short period, he never is the sovereign and chief of the nation. He is never looked up to by the whole people as the head and front of the nation. He is at best but the successful leader of a party. This defect is all the greater on account of the practise of reelection. During his first term of office he is employed in taking steps to secure his own reelection, and for his party a continuance of power. We avoid this by adhering to the monarchical principle— the sovereign whom you respect and love. I believe that it is of the utmost importance to have that principle recognized so that we shall have a sovereign who is placed above the region of party—to whom all parties look up; who is not elevated by the action of one party nor depressed by the action of another; who is the common head and sovereign of all.

With us the sovereign, or in this country the representative of the sovereign, can act only on the advice of his ministers, those ministers being responsible to the people through Parliament. Prior to the formation of the American Union, as we all know, the different States which entered into it were separate Colonies. They had no connection with each other further than that of having a common sovereign, just as with us at present. Their constitutions and their laws were different. They might and did legislate against each other, and when they revolted against the mother country they acted as separate sovereignties and carried on the war by a kind of treaty of alliance against the common enemy. Ever since the Union was formed, the difficulty of what is called "State rights" has existed, and this had much to do in bringing on the present unhappy war in the United States. They commenced, in fact, at the wrong end. They declared by their Constitution that each State was a sovereignty in itself, and that all the powers incident to a sovereignty belonged to each State, except those powers which by the Constitution were conferred upon the general government and Congress.

Here we have adopted a different system. We have strengthened the general government. We have given the general legislature all the great subjects of legislation. We have conferred on them, not only specifically and in detail all the powers which are incident to sovereignty, but we have expressly declared that all subjects of general interest not distinctly and exclusively conferred upon the local governments and local legislatures shall be conferred upon the general government and legislature. We have thus avoided that great source of weakness which has been the cause of the disruption of the United States. We have avoided all conflict of jurisdiction and authority, and if this Constitution is carried out, as it will be in full detail in the imperial act to be passed if the colonies adopt the scheme, we will have in fact, as I said before, all the advantages of a legislative union under one administration, with at the same time the guaranties for local institutions and for local laws which are insisted upon by so many in the Provinces now, I hope, to be united.

I think it is well that in framing our Constitution our first act should have been to recognize the sovereignty of her majesty. I believe that while England has no desire to lose her Colonies, but wishes to retain them—while I am satisfied that the public mind of England would deeply regret the loss of these Provinces—yet, if the people of British North America, after full deliberation, had stated that they considered it was for their interest, for the advantage of the future British North America, to sever the tie, such is the generosity of the people of England that, whatever their desire to keep these Colonies, they would not seek to compel us to remain unwilling subjects of the British Crown. If, therefore, at the conference, we had arrived at the conclusion that it was for the interest of these Provinces that a severance should take place, I am sure that her majesty and the imperial Parliament would have sanctioned that severance. We accordingly felt that there was a propriety in giving a distinct declaration of opinion on that point, and that in framing the Constitution its first sentence should declare that "The executive authority or government shall be vested in the sovereign of the United Kingdom of Great Britain and Ireland, and be administered according to the well-understood principles of the British Constitution, by the sovereign personally, or by the representative of the sovereign duly authorized."

That resolution met with the unanimous assent of the conference. The desire to remain connected with Great Britain and to retain our allegiance to her majesty was unanimous. Not a single suggestion was made that it could by any possibility be for the interest of the Colonies, or of any section or portion of them, that there should be a severance of our connection. Altho we knew it to be possible that Canada, from her position, might be exposed to all the horrors of war by reason of causes of hostility arising between Great Britain and the United States—causes over which we had no control and which we had no hand in bringing about—yet there was a unanimous feeling of willingness to run all the hazards of war, if war must come, rather than lose the connection between the mother country and these Colonies.

We provide that "the executive authority shall be administered by the sovereign personally, or by the representative of the sovereign duly authorized." It is too much to expect that the queen should vouchsafe us her personal governance or presence except to pay us—as the heir-apparent to the throne, our future sovereign, has already paid us—the graceful compliment of a visit. The executive authority must therefore be administered by her majesty's representative. We place no restriction on her majesty's prerogative in the selection of her representative. As it is now, so it will be if this Constitution is adopted. The sovereign has unrestricted freedom of choice. Whether in making her selection, she may send us one of her own family, a royal prince, as a viceroy to rule over us, or one of the

great statesmen of England to represent her,
we know not. We leave that to her majesty in
all confidence. But we may be permitted to
hope that when the union takes place, and we
become the great country which British North
America is certain to be, it will be an object
worthy the ambition of the statesmen of England
to be charged with presiding over our destinies.

CARLYLE

ADDRESS AS LORD RECTOR OF EDINBURGH UNIVERSITY [1]

(1866)

Born in 1795, died in 1881; lived in Scotland until 1834, when he settled in Chelsea, London; Lord Rector of Edinburgh University in 1866, his wife dying in the same year; received the Prussian Order of Merit in 1874; his complete works, in thirty-seven volumes, published in 1872-74.

YOUR enthusiasm toward me, I must admit, is in itself very beautiful, however undeserved it may be in regard to the object of it. It is a feeling honorable to all men, and one well known to myself when I was of an age like yours, nor is it yet quite gone. I can only hope that with you, too, it may endure to the end—this noble desire to honor those whom you think worthy of honor; and that you will come to be more and more select and discriminate in the choice of the object of it—for I can well understand that you will modify your opinions of me and of many things else, as you go on. It is now fifty-six years, gone last November, since I first

---

[1] Delivered on April 2, 1866, and described by Tyndall in a telegram to Mrs. Carlyle, as "a perfect triumph." Abridged. Carlyle went from Edinburgh to his old home in Scotland, and there received news on April 21 of his wife's death while she was driving in Hyde Park, London. By kind permission of Messrs. Chapman and Hall.

entered your city, a boy of not quite fourteen, to attend the classes here, and gain knowledge of all kinds, I could little guess what, my poor mind full of wonder and awe-struck expectation; and now, after a long course, this is what we have come to.

Advices, I believe, to young men, as to all men, are very seldom much valued. There is a great deal of advising, and very little faithful performing; and talk that does not end in any kind of action is better suppressed altogether. I would not, therefore, go much into advising; but there is one advice I must give you. In fact, it is the summary of all advices, and doubtless you have heard it a thousand times; but I must nevertheless let you hear it the thousand-and-first time, for it is most intensely true, whether you will believe it at present or not: namely, that above all things the interest of your whole life depends on your being diligent, now while it is called to-day, in this place where you have come to get education! Diligent: that includes in it all virtues that a student can have; I mean it to include all those qualities of conduct that lead on to the acquirement of real instruction and improvement in such a place.

If you will believe me, you who are young, yours is the golden season of life. As you have heard it called, so it verily is, the seed-time of life; in which, if you do not sow, or if you do sow tares instead of wheat, you can not expect to reap well afterward, and you will arrive at little. And in the course of years, when you come to look back, if you have not done what you have heard from your advisers—and among many counselors there is wisdom—you will bitterly repent when it is too late. The habits of study acquired at universities are of the highest importance in after-life. At the season when you are young in years, the whole mind is, as it were, fluid, and is capable of forming itself into any shape that the owner of the mind pleases to allow it, or constrain it, to form itself into. The mind is then in a plastic or fluid state; but it hardens gradually, to the consistency of rock or of iron, and you can not alter the habits of an old man: he, as he has begun, so he will proceed and go on to the last.

By diligence I mean, among other things, and very chiefly, too—honesty, in all your inquiries, and in all you are about. Pursue your studies in the way your conscience can name honest. More and more endeavor to do that. Keep, I should say for one thing, an accurate separation between what you have really come to know in your minds and what is still unknown. Leave all that latter on the hypothetical side of the barrier, as things afterward to be acquired, if acquired at all; and be careful not to admit a thing as known when you do not yet know it. Count a thing known only when it is imprinted clearly on your mind, and has become transparent to you, so that you may survey it on all sides with intelligence. There is such a thing as a man endeavoring to persuade himself, and endeavoring to persuade others, that he knows things, when he does not know more than the outside skin of them; and yet he goes flourishing about with them.

I dare say you know, very many of you, that it is now some seven hundred years since universities were first set up in this world of ours. Abelard and other thinkers had arisen with doctrines in them which people wished to hear of, and students flocked toward them from all parts of the world. There was no getting the thing recorded in books as you now may. You had to hear the man speaking to you vocally, or else you could not learn at all what it was that he wanted to say. And so they gathered together, these speaking ones—the various people who had anything to teach—and formed themselves gradually, under the patronage of kings and other potentates who were anxious about the culture of their populations, and nobly studious of their best benefit, and became a body corporate, with high privileges, high dignities, and really high aims, under the title of a university.

It remains, however, practically a most important truth, what I alluded to above, that the main use of universities in the present age is that, after you have done with all your classes, the next thing is a collection of books, a great library of good books, which you proceed to study and to read. What the universities can mainly do for you—what I have found the university did for me, is, that it taught me to read, in various languages, in various sciences; so that I could go into the books which treated of these things, and gradually penetrate into any department I wanted to make myself master of, as I found it suit me.

Well, gentlemen, whatever you may think of these historical points, the clearest and most imperative duty lies on every one of you to be assiduous in your reading. Learn to be good readers—which is perhaps a more difficult thing than you imagine. Learn to be discriminative in your reading; to read faithfully, and with your best attention, all kinds of things which you have a real interest in—a real not an imaginary—and which you find to be really fit for what you are engaged in. Of course, at the present time, in a great deal of the reading incumbent on you, you must be guided by the books recommended by your professors for assistance toward the effect of their predilections. And then, when you leave the university, and go into studies of your own, you will find it very important that you have chosen a field, some province specially suited to you, in which you can study and work. The most unhappy of all men is the man who can not tell what he is going to do, who has got no work cut out for him in the world, and does not go into it. For work is the grand cure of all the maladies and miseries that ever beset mankind—honest work, which you intend getting done.

As applicable to all of you, I will say that it is highly expedient to go into history; to inquire into what has passed before you on this earth, and in the family of man.

The history of the Romans and Greeks will first of all concern you; and you will find that the classical knowledge you have got will be extremely applicable to elucidate that. There you have two of the most remarkable races of men in the world set before you, calculated to open innumerable reflections and considerations; a mighty advantage, if you can achieve it—to say nothing of what their two languages will yield you, which your professors can better explain: model languages, which are universally admitted to be the most perfect forms of speech we have yet found to exist among men. And you will find, if you read well, a pair of extremely remarkable nations, shining in the records left by themselves, as a kind of beacon, or solitary mass of illumination, to light up some noble forms of human life for us, in the otherwise utter darkness of the past ages; and it will be well worth your while if you can get into the understanding of what these people were, and what they did. You will find a great deal of hearsay, of empty rumor and tradition, which does not touch on the matter; but perhaps some of you will get to see the old Roman and the old Greek face to face; you will know in some measure how they contrived to exist, and to perform their feats in the world.

I believe, also, you will find one important thing not much noted, that there was a very great deal of deep religion in both nations. This is pointed out by the wiser kind of historians, and particularly by Ferguson, who is very well worth reading on Roman history, and who, I believe, was an alumnus of our own university. His book is a very creditable work. He points out the profoundly religious nature of the Roman people, notwithstanding their ruggedly positive, defiant, and fierce ways. They believed that Jupiter Optimus Maximus was lord of the universe, and that he appointed the Romans to become the chief of nations, provided they followed his commands—to brave all danger, all difficulty, and stand up with an invincible front, and be ready to do and die; and also to have the same sacred regard to truth of promise, to thorough veracity, thorough integrity, and all the virtues that accompany that noblest quality of man, valor—to which latter the Romans gave the name of "virtue" proper (*virtus*, manhood), as the crown and summary of all that is ennobling for a man.

In the literary ages of Rome this religious feeling had very much decayed away; but it still retained its place among the lower classes of the Roman people.

Of the deeply religious nature of the Greeks, along with their beautiful and sunny effulgencies of art, you have striking proof, if you look for it. In the tragedies of Sophocles there is a most deep-toned recognition of the eternal justice of Heaven, and the unfailing punishment of crime against the laws of God. I believe you will find in all histories of nations, that this has been at the origin and foundation of them all; and that no nation which did not contemplate this wonderful universe with an awestricken and reverential belief that there was a great unknown, omnipotent, and all-wise and all-just Being, superintending all men in it, and all interests in it—no nation ever came to very much, nor did any man either, who forgot that. If a man did forget that, he forgot the most important part of his mission in this world.

Our own history of England, which you will naturally take a great deal of pains to make yourselves acquainted with, you will find beyond all others worthy of your study. For indeed I believe that the British nation—including in that the Scottish nation—produced a finer set of men than any you will find it possible to get anywhere else in the world. I do not know, in any history of Greece or Rome, where you will get so fine a man as Oliver Cromwell, for example. And we, too, have had men worthy of memory, in our little corner of the island here, as well as others; and our history has had its heroic features all along and did become great at last in being connected with world-history: for if you examine well, you will find that John Knox was the author, as it were, of Oliver Cromwell; that the Puritan revolution never would

have taken place in England at all, had it not
been for that Scotchman. That is an authentic
fact, and is not prompted by national vanity on
my part, but will stand examining.

I should say also of that protectorate of Oliver Cromwell's, notwithstanding the censures
it has encountered, and the denial of everybody
that it could continue in the world, and so on,
it appears to me to have been, on the whole, the
most salutary thing in the modern history of
England. If Oliver Cromwell had continued
it out, I do not know to what it would have come.
It would have got corrupted probably in other
hands, and could not have gone on; but it was
pure and true, to the last fiber, in his mind;
there was perfect truth in it while he ruled
over it.

Machiavelli has remarked, in speaking of the
Romans, that democracy can not long exist anywhere in the world; that as a mode of government, of national management or administration, it involves an impossibility, and after a
little while must end in wreck. And he goes
on proving that, in his own way. I do not ask
you all to follow him in that conviction—but it
is to him a clear truth; he considers it a solecism
and impossibility that the universal mass of men
should ever govern themselves. He has to admit of the Romans that they continued a long
time, but believes it was purely in virtue of
this item in their constitution—namely, of their
all having the conviction in their minds that it

was solemnly necessary, at times, to appoint a dictator; a man who had the power of life and death over everything, who degraded men out of their places, ordered them to execution, and did whatever seemed to him good in the name of God above him. He was commanded to take care that the Republic suffer no detriment. And Machiavelli calculates that this was the thing which purified the social system from time to time, and enabled it to continue as it did. Probable enough, if you consider it. And an extremely proper function surely, this of a dictator, if the Republic was composed of little other than bad and tumultuous men, triumphing in general over the better, and all going the bad road, in fact. Well, Oliver Cromwell's protectorate, or dictatorate, if you will let me name it so, lasted for about ten years, and you will find that nothing which was contrary to the laws of heaven was allowed to live by Oliver.

One remark more about your reading. I do not know whether it has been sufficiently brought home to you that there are two kinds of books. When a man is reading on any kind of a subject, in most departments of books—in all books, if you take it in a wide sense—he will find that there is a division into good books and bad books. Everywhere a good kind of book and a bad kind of book. I am not to assume that you are unacquainted, or ill acquainted, with this plain fact; but I may remind you that it is becoming a very important consideration in our day. And we have to cast aside altogether the idea people have, that if they are reading any book, that if an ignorant man is reading any book, he is doing rather better than nothing at all. I must entirely call that in question; I even venture to deny that. It would be much safer and better for many a reader, that he had no concern with books at all. There is a number, a frightfully increasing number, of books that are decidedly, to the readers of them, not useful. But an ingenious reader will learn, also, that a certain number of books were written by a supremely noble kind of people—not a very great number of books, but still a number fit to occupy all your reading industry do adhere more or less to that side of things. In short, as I have written it down somewhere else, I conceive that books are like men's souls—divided into sheep and goats. Some few are going up, and carrying us up, heavenward; calculated, I mean, to be of priceless advantage in teaching—in forwarding the teaching of all generations. Others, a frightful multitude, are going down, down; doing ever the more and the wider and the wilder mischief. Keep a strict eye on that latter class of books, my young friends!

And for the rest, in regard to all your studies and readings here, and to whatever you may learn, you are to remember that the object is not particular knowledges,—not that of getting higher and higher in technical perfections, and all that sort of thing. There is a higher aim lying at the rear of all that, especially among those who are intended for literary or speaking pursuits, or the sacred profession. You are ever to bear in mind that there lies behind that the acquisition of what may be called wisdom—namely, sound appreciation and just decision as to all the objects that come round you, and the habit of behaving with justice, candor, clear insight, and loyal adherence to fact. Great is wisdom; infinite is the value of wisdom. It can not be exaggerated; it is the highest achievement of man: "Blessed is he that getteth understanding." And that, I believe, on occasion, may be missed very easily; never more easily than now, I sometimes think. If that is a failure, all is failure! However, I will not touch further upon that matter.

I do not want to discourage any of you from your Demosthenes, and your studies of the niceties of language, and all that. Believe me, I value that as much as any one of you. I consider it a very graceful thing, and a most proper, for every human creature to know what the implement which he uses in communicating his thoughts is, and how to make the very utmost of it. I want you to study Demosthenes, and to know all his excellences. At the same time, I must say that speech, in the case even of Demosthenes, does not seem, on the whole, to have turned to almost any good account. He advised next to nothing that proved practicable; much of the reverse. Why tell me that a man is a fine speaker, if it is not the truth that he is speaking? Phocion,[1] who mostly did not speak at all, was a great deal nearer hitting the mark than Demosthenes. He used to tell the Athenians, "You can't fight Philip. Better if you don't provoke him, as Demosthenes is always urging you to do. You have not the slightest chance with Philip. He is a man who holds his tongue; he has great disciplined armies, a full treasury; he can bribe anybody you like in your cities here; he is going on steadily with an unvarying aim toward his object; while you, with your idle clamorings, with your Cleon the Tanner spouting to you what you take for wisdom! Philip will infallibly beat any set of men such as you, going on raging from shore to shore with all that rampant nonsense." Demosthenes said to him once, "Phocion, you will drive the Athenians mad some day, and they will kill you." "Yes," Phocion answered, "me, when they go mad; and as soon as they get sane again, you!"

The highest outcome and most precious of all the fruits that are to spring from this ideal mode of educating is what Goethe calls art; of which I could at present give no definition that would make it clear to you, unless it were clearer already than is likely. Goethe calls it music, painting, poetry; but it is in quite a higher sense than the common one, and a sense in which, I am

---

[1] Phocion commanded a force which successfully opposed Philip in 339 B.C., but afterward, as leader of the aristocratic party, he advocated peace with Macedon in opposition to Demosthenes.

afraid, most of our painters, poets and music men would not pass muster. He considers this as the highest pitch to which human culture can go—infinitely valuable and ennobling—and he watches with great industry how it is to be brought about in the men who have a turn for it. Very wise and beautiful his notion of the matter is. It gives one an idea that something far better and higher, something as high as ever, and indubitably true, too, is still possible for man in this world. And that is all I can say to you of Goethe's fine theorem of mute education.

Alas, it is painful to think how very far away it all is,—any real fulfilment of such things! For I need not hide from you, young gentlemen, —and it is one of the last things I am going to tell you—that you have got into a very troublous epoch of the world; and I do not think you will find your path in it to be smoother than ours has been, tho you have many advantages which we had not. You have careers open to you, by public examinations and so on, which is a thing much to be approved of and which we hope to see perfected more and more. All that was entirely unknown in my time, and you have many things to recognize as advantages. But you will find the ways of the world, I think, more anarchical than ever. Look where one will, revolution has come upon us. We have got into the age of revolutions. All kinds of things are coming to be subjected to fire, as it were—hotter and hotter blows the element round everything.

Curious to see how, in Oxford and other places that used to seem as lying at anchor in the stream of time, regardless of all changes, they are getting into the highest humor of mutation, and all sorts of new ideas are afloat. It is evident that whatever is not inconsumable, made of asbestos, will have to be burnt in this world. Nothing other will stand the heat it is getting exposed to.

And in saying that, I am but saying in other words that we are in an epoch of anarchy. Anarchy plus a constable! There is nobody that picks one's pocket without some policeman being ready to take him up. But in every other point man is becoming more and more the son, not of cosmos, but of chaos. He is a disobedient, discontented, reckless, and altogether waste kind of object (the commonplace man is, in these epochs); and the wiser kind of man—the select few, of whom I hope you will be a part—has more and more to see to this, to look vigilantly forward, and will require to move with double wisdom; will find, in short, that the crooked things he has got to pull straight in his own life all round him, wherever he may go, are manifold and will task all his strength, however great it be.

But why should I complain of that either? For that is the thing a man is born to in all epochs. He is born to expend every particle of strength that God Almighty has given him, in doing the work he finds he is fit for; to stand up to it to the last breath of life and do his best. We are called upon to do that; and the reward we all get—which we are perfectly sure of, if we have merited it —is that we have got the work done, or at least that we have tried to do the work. For that is a great blessing in itself; and I should say there is not very much more reward than that going in this world. If the man gets meat and clothes, what matter it whether he buy those necessaries with seven thousand a year, or with seven million, could that be, or with seventy pounds a year? He can get meat and clothes for that; and he will find intrinsically, if he is a wise man, wonderfully little real difference.

On the whole, avoid what is called ambition; that is not a fine principle to go upon—and it has in it all degrees of vulgarity, if that is a consideration. "Seekest thou great things, seek them not"; I warmly second that advice of the wisest of men. Do not be ambitious; do not too much need success; be loyal and modest. Cut down the proud towering thoughts that get into you, or see that they be pure as well as high. There is a nobler ambition than the gaining of all California would be, or the getting of all the suffrages that are on the planet just now.

On the whole, I would bid you stand up to your work, whatever it may be, and not be afraid of it; not in sorrows or contradictions to yield, but to push on toward the goal. And do not suppose that people are hostile to you or have you at ill will, in the world. In general, you will rarely find anybody designedly doing you ill. You may feel often as if the whole world were obstructing you, setting itself against you; but you will find that to mean only that the world is traveling in a different way from you, and, rushing on in its own path, heedlessly treads on you. That is mostly all: to you no specific ill will; only each has an extremely good will to himself, which he has a right to have, and is rushing on toward his object. Keep out of literature, I should say also, as a general rule— tho that is by the by. If you find many people who are hard and indifferent to you, in a world which you consider to be inhospitable and cruel—as often indeed happens to a tender-hearted, striving young creature—you will also find there are noble hearts who will look kindly on you; and their help will be precious to you beyond price. You will get good and evil as you go on, and have the success that has been appointed you.

GOLDWIN SMITH

THE SECRET BEYOND SCIENCE[1]

Born in 1823; graduated from Oxford in 1845; Professor of History
in Oxford 1858–66; became Professor in Cornell University in 1868;
removed to Toronto in 1871.

WHAT is the sum of physical science? Compared with the comprehensible universe and with conceivable time, not to speak of infinity and eternity, it is the observation of a mere point, the experience of an instant. Are we warranted in founding anything upon such data, except that which we are obliged to found upon them— the daily rules and processes necessary for the natural life of man? We call the discoveries of science sublime; and truly. But the sublimity belongs not to that which they reveal, but to that which they suggest. And that which they suggest is, that through this material glory and beauty, of which we see a little and imagine more, there speaks to us a being whose nature is akin to ours, and who has made our hearts capable of such converse. Astronomy has its practical uses, without which man's intellect would scarcely rouse itself to those speculations; but

[1] From an address at the University of Oxford entitled "The Study of History." Printed here by kind permission of Messrs. James Parker & Co.

its greatest result is a revelation of immensity pervaded by one informing mind; and this revelation is made by astronomy only in the same sense in which the telescope reveals the stars to the eye of the astronomer.

Science finds no law for the thoughts which, with her aid, are ministered to man by the starry skies. Science can explain the hues of sunset, but she can not tell from what urns of pain and pleasure its pensiveness is poured. These things are felt by all men, felt the more in proportion as the mind is higher. They are a part of human nature; and why should they not be as sound a basis for philosophy as any other part? But if they are, the solid wall of material law melts away, and through the whole order of the material world pours the influence, the personal influence, of a spirit corresponding to our own.

Again, is it true that the fixed or the unvarying is the last revelation of science? These risings in the scale of created beings, this gradual evolution of planetary systems from their center—do they bespeak mere creative force? Do they not rather bespeak something which, for want of an adequate word, we must call creative effort, corresponding to the effort by which man raises himself and his estate? And where effort can be discovered, does not spirit reign again?

A creature whose sphere of vision is a speck, whose experience is a second, sees the pencil of Raphael moving over the canvas of the transfiguration. It sees the pencil moving over its own speck, during its own second of existence, in one particular direction, and it concludes that the formula expressing that direction is the secret of the whole.

There is truth as well as vigor in the lines of Pope on the discoveries of Newton:—

> "Superior beings when of late they saw
> A mortal man unfold all Nature's law,
> Admired such wisdom in the earthly shape,
> And showed a Newton as we show an ape."

If they could not show a Newton as we show an ape, or a Newton's discoveries as we show the feats of apish cunning, it was because Newton was not a mere intellectual power, but a moral being, laboring in the service of his kind, and because his discoveries were the reward, not of sagacity only, but of virtue. We can imagine a mere organ of vision so constructed by omnipotence as to see at a glance infinitely more than could be discovered by all the Newtons, but the animal which possessed that organ would not be higher than the moral being.

Reason, no doubt, is our appointed guide to truth. The limits set to it by each dogmatist, at the point where it comes into conflict with his dogma, are human limits; its providential limits we can learn only by dutifully exerting it to the utmost. Yet reason must be impartial in the acceptance of data and in the demand of proof.

Facts are not the less facts because they are not facts of sense; materialism is not necessarily enlightenment; it is possible to be at once chimerical and gross.

We may venture, without any ingratitude to science as the source of material benefits and the training school of inductive reason, to doubt whether the great secret of the moral world is likely to be discovered in her laboratory, or to be revealed to those minds which have been imbued only with her thoughts, and trained in her processes alone. Some, indeed, among the men of science who have given us sweeping theories of the world, seem to be not only one-sided in their view of the facts, leaving out of sight the phenomena of our moral nature, but to want one of the two faculties necessary for sound investigation. They are acute observers, but bad reasoners. And science must not expect to be exempt from the rules of reasoning. We can not give credit for evidence which does not exist, because if it existed it would be of a scientific kind; nor can we pass at a bound from slight and precarious premises to a tremendous conclusion, because the conclusion would annihilate the spiritual nature and annul the divine origin of man.

BEACONSFIELD

ON THE PRINCIPLES OF HIS PARTY [1]
(1872)

Born in 1804, died in 1881; elected to Parliament in 1837; Chancellor of the Exchequer in 1852, 1858-59, and 1866; carried the Reform Bill in 1867; Prime Minister in 1868, and again in 1874-80; made an Earl in 1876; at the Congress of Berlin in 1878.

I HAVE not come down to Manchester to deliver an essay on the English Constitution; but when the banner of republicanism is unfurled— when the fundamental principles of our institutions are controverted—I think, perhaps, it may not be inconvenient that I should make some few practical remarks upon the character of our Constitution—upon that monarchy limited by the coordinate authority of the estates of the realm, which, under the title of Queen, Lords, and Commons, has contributed so greatly to the prosperity of this country, and with the maintenance of which I believe that prosperity is bound up.

Gentlemen, since the settlement of that Constitution, now nearly two centuries ago, Eng-

[1] Delivered in Manchester in April, 1872, during a widespread discussion, precipitated by Sir Charles Dilke's speech at Newcastle in the previous November denouncing the cost of royalty. Abridged. The result of this discussion was the weakening of the Gladstone ministry, then in power, and finally overthrown two years afterward, Disraeli becoming prime minister. Printed here by kind permission of the London *Times* and Messrs. G. P. Putman's Sons.

land has never experienced a revolution, tho there is no country in which there has been so continuous and such considerable change. How is this? Because the wisdom of your forefathers placed the prize of supreme power without the sphere of human passions. Whatever the struggle of parties, whatever the strife of factions, whatever the excitement and exaltation of the public mind, there has always been something in this country round which all classes and parties could rally, representing the majesty of the law, the administration of justice, and involving, at the same time, the security for every man's rights and the fountain of honor.

Now, gentlemen, it is well clearly to comprehend what is meant by a country not having a revolution for two centuries. It means, for that space, the unbroken exercise and enjoyment of the ingenuity of man. It means for that space the continuous application of the discoveries of science to his comfort and convenience. It means the accumulation of capital, the elevation of labor, the establishment of those admirable factories which cover your district; the unwearied improvement of the cultivation of the land, which has extracted from a somewhat churlish soil harvests more exuberant than those furnished by lands nearer to the sun. It means the continuous order which is the only parent of personal liberty and political right. And you owe all these, gentlemen, to the Throne.

There is another powerful and most beneficial

influence which is also exercised by the Crown. Gentlemen, I am a party man. I believe that, without party, parliamentary government is impossible. I look upon parliamentary government as the noblest government in the world, and certainly the one most suited to England. But without the discipline of political connection, animated by the principle of private honor, I feel certain that a popular assembly would sink before the power or the corruption of a minister. Yet, gentlemen, I am not blind to the faults of party government. It has one great defect. Party has a tendency to warp the intelligence, and there is no minister, however resolved he may be in treating a great public question, who does not find some difficulty in emancipating himself from the traditionary prejudice on which he has long acted. It is, therefore, a great merit in our Constitution, that before a minister introduces a measure to Parliament, he must submit it to an intelligence superior to all party, and entirely free from influences of that character.

I know it will be said, gentlemen, that, however beautiful in theory, the personal influence of the sovereign is now absorbed in the responsibility of the minister. Gentlemen, I think you will find there is great fallacy in this view. The principles of the English Constitution do not contemplate the absence of personal influence on the part of the sovereign; and if they did, the principles of human nature would prevent the fulfilment of such a theory. Gentlemen, I need not tell you that I am now making on this subject abstract observations of general application to our institutions and our history. But take the case of a sovereign of England who accedes to his throne at the earliest age the law permits and who enjoys a long reign—take an instance like that of George III. From the earliest moment of his accession that sovereign is placed in constant communication with the most able statesmen of the period, and of all parties. Even with average ability it is impossible not to perceive that such a sovereign must soon attain a great mass of political information and political experience. Information and experience, gentlemen, whether they are possessed by a sovereign or by the humblest of his subjects, are irresistible in life. No man with the vast responsibility that devolves upon an English minister can afford to treat with indifference a suggestion that has not occurred to him, or information with which he had not been previously supplied.

Gentlemen, the influence of the Crown is not confined merely to political affairs. England is a domestic country. Here the home is revered and the hearth is sacred. The nation is represented by a family—the royal family; and if that family is educated with a sense of responsibility and a sentiment of public duty, it is difficult to exaggerate the salutary influence they may exercise over a nation. It is not merely an influence upon manners; it is not merely that they are a model for refinement and for good taste—they affect the heart as well as the intelligence of the people; and in the hour of public adversity, or in the anxious conjuncture of public affairs, the nation rallies round the family and the throne, and its spirit is animated and sustained by expression of public affection.

Gentlemen, there is yet one other remark that I would make upon our monarchy, tho had it not been for recent circumstances, I should have refrained from doing so. An attack has recently been made upon the Throne on account of the costliness of the institution.[1] Gentlemen, I shall not dwell upon the fact that if the people of England appreciate the monarchy, as I believe they do, it would be painful to them that their royal and representative family should not be maintained with becoming dignity, or fill in the public eye a position inferior to some of the nobles of the land. Nor will I insist upon what is unquestionably the fact, that the revenues of the crown estates, on which our sovereign might live with as much right as the Duke of Bedford, or the Duke of Northumberland, has to his estates, are now paid into the public exchequer. All this, upon the present occasion, I am not going to insist upon. What I now say is this: that there is no sovereignty of any first-rate State which costs so little to the people as the sovereignty of England. I will not compare our civil

---

[1] The speech of Sir Charles Dilke.

list with those of European empires, because it
is known that in amount they treble and quad-
ruple it; but I will compare it with the cost of
sovereignty in a Republic, and that a Republic
with which you are intimately acquainted—the
Republic of the United States of America.

Gentlemen, there is no analogy between the
position of our sovereign, Queen Victoria, and
that of the president of the United States. The
president of the United States is not the sovereign of the United States. There is a very near
analogy between the position of the president of
the United States and that of the prime minister
of England, and both are paid at much the same
rate—the income of a second-class professional
man. The sovereign of the United States is the
people; and I will now show you what the sovereignty of the United States costs. Gentlemen,
you are aware of the Constitution of the United
States. There are thirty-seven independent
States, each with a sovereign Legislature. Besides these, there is a Confederation of States
to conduct their external affairs, which consists
of the House of Representatives and a Senate.
There are two hundred and eighty-five members
of the House of Representatives, and there are
seventy-four members of the Senate, making altogether three hundred and fifty-nine members
of Congress. Now each member of Congress receives 1,000l. sterling per annum. In addition
to this he receives an allowance called "mileage,"
which varies according to the distance which he

travels, but the aggregate cost of which is about 30,000*l.* per annum. That makes 389,000*l.*, almost the exact amount of our civil list.

But this, gentlemen, will allow you to make only a very imperfect estimate of the cost of sovereignty in the United States. Every member of every Legislature in the thirty-seven States is also paid. There are, I believe, 5,010 members of State Legislatures, who receive about $350 per annum each. As some of the returns are imperfect, the average which I have given of expenditure may be rather high, and therefore I have not counted the mileage, which is also universally allowed. Five thousand and ten members of State Legislatures at $350 each make $1,753,500, or 350,700*l.* sterling a year. So you see, gentlemen, that the immediate expenditure for the sovereignty of the United States is between 700,000*l.* and 800,000*l.* a year. Gentlemen, I have not time to pursue this interesting theme, otherwise I could show that you have still but imperfectly ascertained the cost of sovereignty in a Republic.

And now, gentlemen, I would say something on the subject of the House of Lords. It is not merely the authority of the Throne that is now disputed, but the character and influence of the House of Lords that are held up by some to public disregard. Gentlemen, I shall not stop for a moment to offer you any proofs of the advantage of a second chamber, and for this reason: That subject has been discussed now for a century, ever since the establishment of the government of the United States, and all great authorities, American, German, French, Italian, have agreed in this, that a representative government is impossible without a second chamber. And it has been, especially of late, maintained by great political writers in all countries, that the repeated failure of what is called the French Republic is mainly to be ascribed to its not having a second chamber.

But, gentlemen, however anxious foreign countries have been to enjoy this advantage, that anxiety has only been equaled by the difficulty which they have found in fulfilling their object. How is a second chamber to be constituted? By nominees of the sovereign power? What influence can be exercised by a chamber of nominees? Are they to be bound by popular election? In what manner are they to be elected? If by the same constituency as the popular body, what claim have they, under such circumstances, to criticize or to control the decisions of that body? If they are to be elected by a more select body, qualified by a higher franchise, there immediately occurs the objection, why should the majority be governed by the minority? The United States of America were fortunate in finding a solution of this difficulty; but the United States of America had elements to deal with which never occurred before, and never probably will occur again, because they formed their illustrious Senate from materials that were offered them by the thirty-seven States. We, gentlemen, have the House of Lords, an assembly which has historically developed and periodically adapted itself to the wants and necessities of the times.

What, gentlemen, is the first quality which is required in a second chamber? Without doubt, independence. What is the best foundation of independence? Without doubt, property. The prime minister of England has only recently told you, and I believe he spoke quite accurately, that the average income of the members of the House of Lords is 20,000*l.* per annum. Of course there are some who have more, and some who have less; but the influence of a public assembly, so far as property is concerned, depends upon its aggregate property, which, in the present case, is a revenue of 9,000,000*l.* a year. But gentlemen, you must look to the nature of this property. It is visible property, and therefore it is responsible property, which every ratepayer in the room knows to his cost. But, gentlemen, it is not only visible property; it is, generally speaking, territorial property, and one of the elements of territorial property is, that it is representative.

Gentlemen, it is said that the diminished power of the Throne and the assailed authority of the House of Lords are owing to the increased power of the House of Commons, and the new position which of late years, and especially during the last forty years, it has assumed in the English

Constitution. Gentlemen, the main power of the House of Commons depends upon its command over the public purse, and its control of the public expenditure; and if that power is possessed by a party which has a large majority in the House of Commons, the influence of the House of Commons is proportionately increased, and, under some circumstances, becomes more predominant. But, gentlemen, this power of the House of Commons is not a power which has been created by any reform act, from the days of Lord Grey in 1832 to 1867. It is the power which the House of Commons has enjoyed for centuries, which it has frequently asserted and sometimes even tyrannically exercised. Gentlemen, the House of Commons represents the constituencies of England, and I am here to show you that no addition to the elements of that constituency has placed the House of Commons in a different position with regard to the Throne and the House of Lords from that it has always constitutionally occupied.

Gentlemen, we speak now on this subject with great advantage. We recently have had published authentic documents upon this matter which are highly instructive. We have, for example, just published the census of Great Britain, and we are now in possession of the last registration of voters for the United Kingdom. Gentlemen, it appears that by the census the population at this time is about 32,-000,000. It is shown by the last registration, that after making the usual deductions for deaths, removals, double entries, and so on, the constituency of the United Kingdom may be placed at 2,200,000. So, gentlemen, it at once appears that there are 30,000,000 people in this country who are as much represented by the House of Lords as by the House of Commons, and who, for the protection of their rights, must depend upon them and the majesty of the Throne.

But, gentlemen, the Constitution of England is not merely a constitution in State; it is a constitution in Church and State. The wisest sovereigns and statesmen have ever been anxious to connect authority with religion—some to increase their power, some, perhaps, to mitigate its exercise. But the same difficulty has been experienced in effecting this union which has been experienced in forming a second chamber—either the spiritual power has usurped upon the civil, and established a sacerdotal society, or the civil power has invaded successfully the rights of the spiritual, and the ministers of religion have been degraded into stipendiaries of the State and instruments of the government. In England we accomplish this great result by an alliance between Church and State, between two originally independent powers. I will not go into the history of that alliance, which is rather a question for those archæological societies which occasionally amuse and instruct the people of this city. Enough for me that this union was made and has contributed for centuries to the civilization of this country. Gentlemen, there is the same assault against the Church of England and the union between the State and the Church as there is against the monarchy and against the House of Lords. It is said that the existence of nonconformity proves that the Church is a failure. I draw from these premises an exactly contrary conclusion; and I maintain that to have secured a national profession of faith with the unlimited enjoyment of private judgment in matters spiritual, is the solution of the most difficult problem, and one of the triumphs of civilization.

It is said that the existence of parties in the Church also proves its incompetence. On that matter, too, I entertain a contrary opinion. Parties have always existed in the Church; and some have appealed to them as arguments in favor of its divine institution, because, in the services and doctrines of the Church have been found representatives of every mood in the human mind. Those who are influenced by ceremonies find consolation in forms which secure to them the beauty of holiness. Those who are not satisfied except with enthusiasm find in its ministrations the exaltation they require, while others who believe that the "anchor of faith" can never be safely moored except in the dry sands of reason find a religion within the pale of the Church which can boast of its irrefragable logic and its irresistible evidence.

Gentlemen, I am inclined sometimes to believe that those who advocate the abolition of the union between Church and State have not carefully considered the consequences of such a course. The Church is a powerful corporation of many millions of her majesty's subjects, with a consummate organization and wealth which in its aggregate is vast. Restricted and controlled by the State, so powerful a corporation may be only fruitful of public advantage, but it becomes a great question what might be the consequences of the severance of the controlling tie between these two bodies. The State would be enfeebled, but the Church would probably be strengthened. Whether that is a result to be desired is a grave question for all men. For my own part, I am bound to say that I doubt whether it would be favorable to the cause of civil and religious liberty.

But, gentlemen, after all, the test of political institutions is the condition of the country whose fortunes they regulate; and I do not mean to evade that test. You are the inhabitants of an island of no collossal size, which, geographically speaking, was intended by nature as the appendage of some continental empire—either of Gauls and Franks on the other side of the Channel, or of Teutons and Scandinavians beyond the German Sea. Such indeed, and for a long period, was your early history. You were invaded; you were pillaged and you were conquered; yet amid all these disgraces and vicissitudes there was gradually formed that English race which has brought about a very different state of affairs. Instead of being invaded, your land is proverbially the only "inviolate land"— "the inviolate land of the sage and free." Instead of being plundered, you have attracted to your shores all the capital of the world. Instead of being conquered, your flag floats on many waters, and your standard waves in either zone. It may be said that these achievements are due to the race that inhabited the land, and not to its institutions. Gentlemen, in political institutions are the embodied experiences of a race. You have established a society of classes which give vigor and variety to life. But no class possesses a single exclusive privilege, and all are equal before the law. You possess a real aristocracy, open to all who desire to enter it. You have not merely a middle class, but a hierarchy of middle classes, in which every degree of wealth, refinement, industry, energy, and enterprise is duly represented.

And now, gentlemen, what is the condition of the great body of the people? In the first place, gentlemen, they have for centuries been in the full enjoyment of that which no other country in Europe has ever completely attained —complete rights of personal freedom. In the second place, there has been a gradual, and therefore a wise, distribution on a large scale of political rights. Speaking with reference to the industries of this great part of the country,

I can personally contrast it with the condition of the working classes forty years ago. In that period they have attained two results—the raising of their wages and the diminution of their toil. Increased means and increased leisure are the two civilizers of man. That the working classes of Lancashire and Yorkshire have proved not unworthy of these boons may be easily maintained; but their progress and elevation have been during this interval wonderfully aided and assisted by three causes, which are not so distinctively attributable to their own energies. The first is the revolution in locomotion, which has opened the world to the working man, which has enlarged the horizon of his experience, increased his knowledge of nature and of art, and added immensely to the salutary recreation, amusement, and pleasure of his existence. The second cause is the cheap postage, the moral benefits of which can not be exaggerated. And the third is that unshackled Press which has furnished him with endless sources of instruction, information, and amusement.

But now, gentlemen, I want to test the condition of the agricultural laborer generally; and I will take a part of England with which I am familiar, and can speak as to the accuracy of the facts—I mean the group described as the south-midland counties. The conditions of labor there are the same, or pretty nearly the same, throughout. The group may be described as a strictly agricultural community, and they embrace a pop-

ulation of probably a million and a half. Now,
I have no hesitation in saying that the improvement in their lot during the last forty years has
been progressive and is remarkable. I attribute
it to three causes: In the first place, the rise in
their money wages is no less than fifteen per
cent. The second great cause of their improvement is the almost total disappearance of excessive and exhausting toil, from the general
introduction of machinery. I do not know
whether I could get a couple of men who could
or, if they could, would thresh a load of wheat
in my neighborhood. The third great cause
which has improved their condition is the very
general, not to say universal, institution of allot-
ment grounds.

Now, gentlemen, when I find that this has
been the course of affairs in our very considerable
and strictly agricultural portion of the country,
where there have been no exceptional circumstances, like smuggling, to degrade and demoral-
ize the race, I can not resist the conviction that
the condition of the agricultural laborers, instead
of being stationary, as we are constantly told
by those not acquainted with them, has been
one of progressive improvement, and that in
those counties—and they are many—where the
stimulating influence of a manufacturing neighborhood acts upon the land, the general conclusion at which I arrive is that the agricultural
laborer has had his share in the advance of national prosperity.

Gentlemen, I am not here to maintain that there is nothing to be done to increase the well-being of the working classes of this country, generally speaking. There is not a single class in the country which is not susceptible of improvement; and that makes the life and animation of our society. But in all we do we must remember, as my noble friend told them at Liverpool, that much depends upon the working classes themselves; and what I know of the working classes in Lancashire makes me sure that they will respond to this appeal. Much also may be expected from that sympathy between classes which is a distinctive feature of the present day; and, in the last place, no inconsiderable results may be obtained by judicious and prudent legislation. But, gentlemen, in attempting to legislate upon social matters, the great object is to be practical—to have before us some distinct aims and some distinct means by which they can be accomplished.

Gentlemen, I can not pretend that our position either at home or abroad is in my opinion satisfactory. At home, at a period of immense prosperity, with a people contented and naturally loyal, we find to our surprise the most extravagant doctrines professed and the fundamental principles of our most valuable institutions impugned, and that, too, by persons of some authority. Gentlemen, this startling inconsistency is accounted for, in my mind, by the circumstances under which the present administration was formed. It is the first instance in my knowledge of a British administration being avowedly formed on a principle of violence. It is unnecessary for me to remind you of the circumstances which preceded the formation of that government. You were the principal scene and theater of the development of statesmanship that then occurred. You witnessed the incubation of the portentous birth. You remember when you were informed that the policy to secure the prosperity of Ireland and the content of Irishmen was a policy of sacrilege and confiscation. Gentlemen, when Ireland was placed under the wise and able administration of Lord Abercorn, Ireland was prosperous, and I may say content. But there happened at that time a very peculiar conjuncture in politics. The civil war in America had just ceased; and a band of military adventurers—Poles, Italians, and many Irishmen—concocted in New York a conspiracy [1] to invade Ireland, with the belief that the whole country would rise to welcome them. How that conspiracy was baffled—how those plots were confounded, I need not now remind you. For that we were mainly indebted to the eminent qualities of a great man who has just left us.[2] You remember how the constituencies were appealed to to vote against the government which had made so unfit an appointment as that of Lord Mayo to the viceroyalty of India.

[1] The Fenian movement to secure the independence of Ireland.
[2] Lord Mayo, who, as viceroy of India, was assassinated in 1872.

It was by his great qualities when secretary for Ireland, by his vigilance, his courage, his patience, and his perseverance that this conspiracy was defeated. Never was a minister better informed. He knew what was going on at New York just as well as what was going on in the City of Dublin.

When the Fenian conspiracy had been entirely put down, it became necessary to consider the policy which it was expedient to pursue in Ireland; and it seemed to us at that time that what Ireland required after all the excitement which it had experienced was a policy which should largely develop its material resources. There were one or two subjects of a different character, which, for the advantage of the State, it would have been desirable to have settled, if that could have been effected with a general concurrence of both the great parties in that country. Had we remained in office, that would have been done. But we were destined to quit it, and we quitted it without a murmur. The policy of our successors was different. Their specific was to despoil churches and plunder landlords, and what has been the result? Sedition rampant, treason thinly veiled, and whenever a vacancy occurs in the representation a candidate is returned pledged to the disruption of the realm. Her majesty's new ministers proceeded in their career like a body of men under the influence of some delirious drug. Not satiated with the spoliation and anarchy of Ireland, they began to attack every institution and every interest, every class and calling in the country.

It is curious to observe their course. They took into hand the army. What have they done? I will not comment on what they have done. I will historically state it, and leave you to draw the inference. So long as constitutional England has existed there has been a jealousy among all classes against the existence of a standing army. As our Empire expanded, and the existence of a large body of disciplined troops became a necessity, every precaution was taken to prevent the danger to our liberties which a standing army involved.

It was a first principle not to concentrate in the island any overwhelming number of troops, and a considerable portion was distributed in the Colonies. Care was taken that the troops generally should be officered by a class of men deeply interested in the property and the liberties of England. So extreme was the jealousy, that the relations between that once constitutional force, the militia, and the sovereign were rigidly guarded, and it was carefully placed under local influences. All this is changed. We have a standing army of large amount, quartered and brigaded and encamped permanently in England, and fed by a considerable and constantly increasing reserve.

I will illustrate this point by two anecdotes. Since I have been in public life there has been for this country a great calamity and there is a great danger, and both might have been avoided. The calamity was the Crimean War. You know what were the consequences of the Crimean War: a great addition to your debt, an enormous addition to your taxation, a cost more precious than your treasure—the best blood of England. Half a million of men, I believe, perished in that great undertaking. Nor are the evil consequences of that war adequately described by what I have said. All the disorders and disturbances of Europe, those immense armaments that are an incubus on national industry and the great obstacle to progressive civilization, may be traced and justly attributed to the Crimean War. And yet the Crimean War need never have occurred.

The great danger is the present state of our relations with the United States.[1] When I acceded to office, I did so, so far as regarded the United States of America, with some advantage. During the whole of the Civil War in America both my noble friend near me [2] and I had maintained a strict and fair neutrality. This was fully appreciated by the government of the United States, and they expressed their wish that with our aid the settlement of all differences between the two governments should be accomplished. They sent here a plenipotentiary, an honorable gentleman, very intelligent and possessing general confidence. My noble friend

---

[1] In the matter of the Alabama Claims.

[2] Lord Derby, then Lord Stanley.

near me, with great ability, negotiated a treaty
for the settlement of all these claims. He was
the first minister who proposed to refer them
to arbitration, and the treaty was signed by the
American government. It was signed, I think,
on November 10th, on the eve of the dissolution
of Parliament. The borough elections that first
occurred proved what would be the fate of the
ministry, and the moment they were known in
America the American government announced
that Mr. Reverdy Johnson [the American Minis-
ter] had mistaken his instructions, and they
could not present the treaty to the Senate for its
sanction—the sanction of which there had been
previously no doubt.

But the fact is that, as in the case of the Crimean War, it was supposed that our successors
would be favorable to Russian aggression, so it
was supposed that by the accession to office of
Mr. Gladstone and a gentleman you know well,
Mr. Bright, the American claims would be considered in a very different spirit. How they
have been considered is a subject which, no doubt,
occupies deeply the minds of the people of Lancashire. Now, gentlemen, observe this—the
question of the Black Sea involved in the Crimean War, the question of the American Claims
involved in our negotiations with Mr. Johnson,[1]
are the two questions that have again turned

[1] Reverdy Johnson, the American minister to England in 1868–69,
who negotiated a treaty for the settlement of the Alabama Claims,
which was rejected by the Senate.

up, and have been the two great questions that have been under the management of the government.

I come now to that question which most deeply interests you at this moment, and that is our relations with the United States. I approved the government referring this question to arbitration. It was only following the policy of Lord Stanley. My noble friend disapproved the negotiations being carried on at Washington. I confess that I would willingly have persuaded myself that this was not a mistake, but reflection has convinced me that my noble friend was right. I remember the successful negotiation of the Clayton-Bulwer Treaty by Sir Henry Bulwer. I flattered myself that treaties at Washington might be successfully negotiated; but I agree with my noble friend that his general view was far more sound than my own. But no one, when that commission was sent forth, for a moment could anticipate the course of their conduct under the strict injunctions of the government. We believed that commission was sent to ascertain what points should be submitted to arbitration, to be decided by the principles of the law of nations. We had not the slightest idea that that commission was sent with power and instructions to alter the law of nations itself. When that result was announced, we expressed our entire disapprobation; and yet trusting to the representations of the government that matters were concluded satisfactorily, we had to decide whether it were wise, if the great result was obtained, to wrangle upon points, however important, such as those to which I have referred.

Gentlemen, it appears that, tho all parts of England were ready to make those sacrifices, the two negotiating States—the government of the United Kingdom and the government of the United States—placed a different interpretation upon the treaty when the time had arrived to put its provisions into practise. Gentlemen, in my mind, and in the opinion of my noble friend near me, there was but one course to take under the circumstances, painful as it might be, and that was at once to appeal to the good feeling and good sense of the United States, and, stating the difficulty, to invite confidential conference whether it might not be removed. But her majesty's government took a different course. On December 15th her majesty's government were aware of a contrary interpretation being placed on the Treaty of Washington by the American government. The prime minister received a copy of their counter case, and he confessed he had never read it. He had a considerable number of copies sent to him to distribute among his colleags, and you remember, probably, the remarkable statement in which he informed the House that he had distributed those copies to everybody except those for whom they were intended.

Time went on, and the adverse interpretation

of the American government oozed out, and was noticed by the Press. Public alarm and public indignation were excited; and it was only seven weeks afterward, on the very eve of the meeting of Parliament—some twenty-four hours before the meeting of Parliament—that her majesty's government felt they were absolutely obliged to make a "friendly communication" to the United States that they had arrived at an interpretation of the treaty the reverse of that of the American government. What was the position of the American government? Seven weeks had passed without their having received the slightest intimation from her majesty's ministers. They had circulated their case throughout the world. They had translated it into every European language. It had been sent to every court and cabinet, to every sovereign and prime minister. It was impossible for the American government to recede from their position, even if they had believed it to be an erroneous one. And then, to aggravate the difficulty, the prime minister goes down to Parliament, declares that there is only one interpretation to be placed on the treaty, and defies and attacks everybody who believes it susceptible of another.

Was there ever such a combination of negligence and blundering? And now, gentlemen, what is about to happen? All we know is that her majesty's ministers are doing everything in their power to evade the cognizance and criticism of Parliament. They have received an answer to their "friendly communication," of which, I believe, it has been ascertained that the American government adhere to their interpretation; and yet they prolong the controversy. What is about to occur it is unnecessary for one to predict; but if it be this—if after a fruitless ratiocination worthy of a schoolman, we ultimately agree so far to the interpretation of the American government as to submit the whole case to arbitration, with feeble reservation of a protest, if it be decided against us, I venture to say that we shall be entering on a course not more distinguished by its feebleness than by its impending peril. There is before us every prospect of the same incompetence that distinguished our negotiations respecting the independence of the Black Sea; and I fear that there is every chance that this incompetence will be sealed by our ultimately asknowledging these direct claims of the United States, which, both as regards principle and practical results, are fraught with the utmost danger to this country.

Gentlemen, do not suppose, because I counsel firmness and decision at the right moment, that I am of that school of statesmen who are favorable to a turbulent and aggressive diplomacy. I have resisted it during a great part of my life. I am not unaware that the relations of England to Europe have undergone a vast change during the century that has just elapsed. The relations of England to Europe are not the same as they were in the days of Lord Chatham or Frederick the Great. The queen of England has become the sovereign of the most powerful of Oriental States. On the other side of the globe there are now establishments belonging to her, teeming with wealth and population, which will, in due time, exercise their influence over the distribution of power. The old establishments of this country, now the United States of America, throw their lengthening shades over the Atlantic, which mix with European waters. These are vast and novel elements in the distribution of power. I acknowledge that the policy of England with respect to Europe should be a policy of reserve, but proud reserve; and in answer to those statesmen—those mistaken statesmen who have intimated the decay of the power of England and the decline of its resources—I express here my confident conviction that there never was a moment in our history when the power of England was so great and her resources so vast and inexhaustible.

And yet, gentlemen, it is not merely our fleets and armies, our powerful artillery, our accumulated capital, and our unlimited credit on which I so much depend, as upon that unbroken spirit of her people, which I believe was never prouder of the imperial country to which they belong. Gentlemen, it is to that spirit that I above all things trust. I look upon the people of Lancashire as a fair representative of the people of England. I think the manner in which they have invited me here, locally a stranger, to receive the expression of their cordial sympathy, and only because they recognize some effort on my part to maintain the greatness of their country, is evidence of the spirit of the land. I must express to you again my deep sense of the generous manner in which you have welcomed me, and in which you have permitted me to express to you my views upon public affairs. Proud of your confidence, and encouraged by your sympathy, I now deliver to you, as my last words, the cause of the Tory party, the English Constitution, and of the British Empire.

GLADSTONE

ON THE DOMESTIC AND FOREIGN AFFAIRS
OF ENGLAND [1]

(1879)

Born in 1809, died in 1898; first elected to Parliament in 1832;
Vice-President of the Board of Trade in 1841 and President in 1843;
Colonial Secretary in 1846; Chancellor of the Exchequer in 1852,
1855, and 1859; Prime Minister in 1868 and three times subsequently
until 1894; with the exception of a year and a half sat continuously
in the House from 1832 until 1895.

GENTLEMEN, I speak of agricultural distress
as a matter now undoubtedly serious. Let none
of us withhold our sympathy from the farmer,
the cultivator of the soil, in the struggle he has
to undergo. His struggle is a struggle of competition with the United States. But I do not
fully explain the case when I say the United
States. It is not with the entire United States,
it is with the western portion of these States—
that portion remote from the seaboard; and I
wish in the first place, gentlemen, to state to
you all a fact of very great interest and importance, as it seems to me, relating to and defining
the point at which the competition of the West-

---

[1] Delivered during his Midlothian campaign, November 27, 1879,
and followed by his return to power as prime minister in the following spring, succeeding Beaconsfield. Abridged. By kind permission of the London *Times* and Messrs. G. P. Putnam's Sons.

ern States of America is most severely felt. Whatever be agricultural distress in Scotland, whatever it be, where undoubtedly it is more felt, in England, it is greater by much in the Eastern States of America. In the States of New England the soil has been to some extent exhausted by careless methods of agriculture, and these, gentlemen, are the greatest of all enemies with which the farmer has to contend.

But the foundation of the statement I make, that the Eastern States of America are those that most feel the competition of the West, is to be found in facts—in this fact above all, that not only they are not in America, as we are here, talking about the shortness of the annual returns, and in some places having much said on the subject of rents, and of temporary remission or of permanent reduction. That is not the state of things; they have actually got to this point, that the capital values of land, as tested by sales in the market, have undergone an enormous diminution.

There has been developed in the astonishing progressive power of the United States—there has been developed a faculty of producing corn[1] for the subsistence of man, with a rapidity and to an extent unknown in the experience of mankind. There is nothing like it in history. Do not let us conceal, gentlemen, from ourselves the fact; I shall not stand the worst with any of you who are farmers if I at once avow that

---

[1] Used here in the English sense as meaning wheat.

this greater and comparatively immense abundance of the prime article of subsistence for mankind is a great blessing vouchsafed by Providence to mankind. In part I believe that the cheapness has been increased by special causes. The lands from which the great abundance of American wheat comes are very thinly peopled as yet. They will become more thickly peopled, and as they become more thickly peopled a larger proportion of their produce will be wanted for home consumption and less of it will come to you, and at a higher price.

Again, if we are rightly informed, the price of American wheat has been unnaturally reduced by the extraordinary depression, in recent times, of trade in America, and especially of the mineral trades, upon which many railroads are dependent in America, and with which these railroads are connected in America in a degree and manner that in this country we know but little of. With a revival of trade in America it is to be expected that the freights of corn will increase, and all other freights, because the employment of the railroads will be a great deal more abundant, and they will not be content to carry corn at nominal rates. In some respects, therefore, you may expect a mitigation of the pressure, but in other respects it is likely to continue.

How are you to meet that state of things? What are your fair claims? I will tell you. In my opinion your fair claims are, in the main, two. One is to be allowed to purchase every article that you require in the cheapest market, and have no needless burden laid upon anything that comes to you and can assist you in the cultivation of your land. But that claim has been conceded and fulfilled.

I do not know whether there is an object, an instrument, a tool of any kind, an auxiliary of any kind, that you want for the business of the farmer, which you do not buy at this moment in the cheapest market. But beyond that, you want to be relieved from every unjust and unnecessary legislative restraint. I say every unnecessary legislative restraint, because taxation, gentlemen, is unfortunately a restraint upon us all, but we can not say that it is always unnecessary, and we can not say that it is always unjust. Yesterday I ventured to state—and I will therefore not now return to the subject— a number of matters connected with the state of legislation in which it appears to me to be of vital importance, both to the agricultural interest and to the entire community, that the occupiers and cultivators of the land of this country should be relieved from restraints under the operation of which they now suffer considerably. Beyond those two great heads, gentlemen, what you have to look to, I believe, is your own energy, your own energy of thought and action, and your care not to undertake to pay rents greater than, in reasonable calculation, you think you can afford.

There are some gentlemen, and there are persons for whom I for one have very great respect, who think that the difficulties of our agriculture may be got over by a fundamental change in the landholding system of this country.

I do not mean, now pray observe, a change as to the law of entail and settlement, and all those restraints which, I hope, were tolerably well disposed of yesterday at Dalkeith; but I mean those who think that if you can cut up the land, or a large part of it, into a multitude of small properties, that of itself will solve the difficulty, and start everybody on a career of prosperity.

Now, gentlemen, to a proposal of that kind, I, for one, am not going to object upon the ground that it would be inconsistent with the privileges of landed proprietors. In my opinion, if it is known to be for the welfare of the community at large, the legislature is perfectly entitled to buy out the landed proprietors. It is not intended probably to confiscate the property of a landed proprietor more than the property of any other man; but the State is perfectly entitled, if it please, to buy out the landed proprietors as it may think fit, for the purpose of dividing the property into small lots. I do not wish to recommend it, because I will show you the doubts that, to my mind, hang about that proposal; but I admit that on principle no objection can be taken. Those persons who possess large portions of the spaces of the earth are not altogether in the same position as the possessors of mere personalty; that personalty does not impose the same limitations upon the action and industry of man, and upon the well-being of the community, as does the possession of land; and, therefore, I freely own that compulsory expropriation is a thing which for an adequate public object is in itself admissible and so far sound in principle.

Now, gentlemen, this idea about small proprietors, however, is one which very large bodies and parties in this country treat with the utmost contempt; and they are accustomed to point to France, and say: "Look at France." In France you have got five millions—I am not quite sure whether it is five millions or more; I do not wish to be beyond the mark in anything—you have five millions of small proprietors, and you do not produce in France as many bushels of wheat per acre as you do in England. Well, now I am going to point out to you a very remarkable fact with regard to the condition of France. I will not say that France produces—for I believe it does not produce—as many bushels of wheat per acre as England does, but I should like to know whether the wheat of France is produced mainly upon the small properties of France. I believe that the wheat of France is produced mainly upon the large properties of France, and I have not any doubt that the large properties of England are, upon the whole, better cultivated, and more capital is put into the land than in the large properties of France.

But it is fair that justice should be done to what is called the peasant proprietary. Peasant proprietary is an excellent thing, if it can be had, in many points of view. It interests an enormous number of the people in the soil of the country, and in the stability of its institutions and its laws. But now look at the effect that it has upon the progressive value of the land—and I am going to give you a very few figures which I will endeavor to relieve from all complication, lest I should unnecessarily weary you. But what will you think when I tell you that the agricultural value of France— the taxable income derived from the land, and therefore the income of the proprietors of that land—has advanced during our lifetime far more rapidly than that of England? When I say England I believe the same thing is applicable to Scotland, certainly to Ireland; but I shall take England for my test, because the difference between England and Scotland, tho great, does not touch the principle, and, because it so happens that we have some means of illustration from former times for England, which are not equally applicable for all the three kingdoms.

Here is the state of the case. I will not go back any farther than 1851. I might go back much farther; it would only strengthen my case. But for 1851 I have a statement made by French official authority of the agricultural income of France, as well as the income of other real property, viz., houses. In 1851 the agricultural income of France was 76,000,000*l.* It was greater in 1851 than the whole income from land and houses together had been in 1821. This is a tolerable evidence of progress; but I will not enter into the detail of it, because I have no means of dividing the two—the house income and the land income—for the earlier year, namely, 1821. In 1851 it was 76,000,000*l.* —the agricultural income; and in 1864 it had risen from 76,000,000*l.* to 106,000,000*l.* That is to say, in the space of thirteen years the increase of agricultural values in France—annual values—was no less than forty per cent., or three per cent. per annum. Now, I go to England. Wishing to be quite accurate, I shall limit myself to that with respect to which we have positive figures. In England the agricultural income in 1813-14 was 37,000,000*l.*; in 1842 it was 42,000,000*l.*, and that year is the one I will take as my starting point. I have given you the years 1851 to 1864 in France. I could only give you those thirteen years with a certainty that I was not misleading you, and I believe I have kept within the mark. I believe I might have put my case more strongly for France.

In 1842, then, the agricultural income of England was 42,000,000*l.*; in 1876 it was 52,-

000,000*l.*—that is to say, while the agricultural income of France increased forty per cent. in thirteen years, the agricultural income of England increased twenty per cent. in thirty-four years. The increase in France was three per cent. per annum; the increase in England was about one-half or three-fifths per cent. per annum. Now, gentlemen, I wish this justice to be done to a system where peasant proprietary prevails. It is of great importance. And will you allow me, you who are Scotch agriculturists, to assure you that I speak to you not only with the respect which is due from a candidate to a constituency, but with the deference which is due from a man knowing very little of agricultural matters to those who know a great deal? And there is one point at which the considerations that I have been opening up, and this rapid increase of the value of the soil in France, bear upon our discussions. Let me try to explain it. I believe myself that the operation of economic laws is what in the main dictates the distribution of landed property in this country. I doubt if those economic laws will allow it to remain cut up into a multitude of small properties like the small properties of France. As to small holdings, I am one of those who attach the utmost value to them. I say that in the Lothians—I say that in the portion of the country where almost beyond any other large holdings prevail—in some parts of which large holdings exclusively are to be found—I attach the utmost value to them. But it is not on that point I am going to dwell, for we have no time for what is unnecessary. What I do wish very respectfully to submit to you, gentlemen, is this:

When you see this vast increase of the agricultural value of France, you know at once it is perfectly certain that it has not been upon the large properties of France, which, if anything, are inferior in cultivation to the large properties of England. It has been upon those very peasant-properties which some people are so ready to decry. What do the peasant-properties mean? They mean what, in France, is called the small cultivation—that is to say, cultivation of superior articles, pursued upon a small scale—cultivation of flowers, cultivation of trees and shrubs, cultivation of fruits of every kind, and all that, in fact, which rises above the ordinary character of farming produce, and rather approaches the produce of the gardener.

But I go on to another remedy which is proposed, and I do it with a great deal less of respect; nay, I now come to the region of what I have presumed to call quack remedies. There is a quack remedy which is called reciprocity, and this quack remedy is under the special protection of quack doctors, and among the quack doctors, I am sorry to say, there appear to be some in very high station indeed; and if I am rightly informed, no less a person than her majesty's secretary of state for foreign affairs has been moving about the country, and indicating a very considerable expectation that possibly by reciprocity agricultural distress will be relieved. Let me test, gentlemen, the efficacy of this quack remedy for your, in some places, agricultural pressure, and generally distress—the pressure that has been upon you, the struggle in which you are engaged. Pray watch its operation; pray note what is said by the advocates of reciprocity. They always say, We are the soundest and best free-traders. We recommend reciprocity because it is the truly effectual method of bringing about free trade. At present America imposes enormous duties upon our cotton goods and upon our iron goods. Put reciprocity into play, and America will become a free-trading country. Very well, gentlemen, how would that operate upon you agriculturists in particular? Why, it would operate thus: If your condition is to be regretted in certain particulars, and capable of amendment, I beg you to cast an eye of sympathy upon the condition of the American agriculturist. It has been very well said, and very truly said,—tho it is a smart antithesis—the American agriculturist has got to buy everything that he wants at prices which are fixed in Washington by the legislation of America, but he has got to sell everything that he produces at prices which are fixed in Liverpool—fixed by the free competition of the world. How would you like that, gentlemen,—to have protective prices to pay for everything that you use—for your manures, for your animals, for your implements, for all your farming stock, and at the same time to have to sell what you produce in the free and open market of the world?

But, gentlemen, there is another set of men who are bolder still, and who are not for reciprocity; who are not content with that milder form of quackery, but who recommend a reversion, pure and simple, to what I may fairly call, I think, the exploded doctrine of protection.

Some of the members of her majesty's government—the minor members of her majesty's government—the humbler luminaries of that great constellation—have been going about the country and telling their farming constituents that they think the time has come when a return to protection might very wisely be tried. But, gentlemen, what delusions have been practised upon the unfortunate British farmer! When we go back for twenty years, what is now called the Tory party was never heard of as the Tory party. It was always heard of as the party of protection. As long as the chiefs of the protective party were not in office, as long as they were irresponsible, they recommended themselves to the good will of the farmer as Protectionists, and said they would set him up and put his interests on a firm foundation through protection. We brought them into office in the year 1852. I gave with pleasure a vote that assisted to bring them into office. I thought bringing them into office was the only way of putting their professions to the test. They came into office, and before they had been six months in office they had thrown protection to the winds. And that is the way in which the British farmer's expectations are treated by those who claim for themselves in the special sense the designation of his friends.

But are we such children that, after spending twenty years—as I may say from 1840 to 1860 —in breaking down the huge fabric of protection, in 1879 we are seriously to set about building it up again? If that be right, gentlemen, let it be done, but it will involve on our part a most humiliating confession. In my opinion it is not right. Protection, however, let me point out, now is asked for in two forms, and I am next going to quote Lord Beaconsfield for the purpose of expressing my concurrence with him.

Since 1842, and down to the present time, we have had along with railways—always increasing their benefits—we have had the successive adoption of free-trade measures; and what has been the state of the export business of the country? It has risen in this degree, that that which from 1840 to 1842 averaged 50,000,-000*l.*, from 1873 to 1878 averaged 218,000,000*l.* Instead of increasing, as it had done between 1830 and 1842, when railways only were at work, at the rate of 1,000,000*l.* a year—instead of remaining stagnant as it did when the country was under protection pure and simple, with no augmentation of the export trade to enlarge the means of those who buy your products, the total growth in a period of thirty-five years was no less than 168,000,000*l*., or taking it roughly, a growth in the export trade of the country to the extent of between 4,000,000*l*. and 5,000,000*l*. a year. But, gentlemen, you know the fact. You know very well, that while restriction was in force, you did not get the prices that you have been getting for the last twenty years. The price of wheat has been much the same as it had been before. The price of oats is a better price than was to be had on the average of protective times. But the price, with the exception of wheat, of almost every agricultural commodity, the price of wool, the price of meat, the price of cheese, the price of everything that the soil produces, has been largely increased in a market free and open to the world; because, while the artificial advantage which you got through protection, as it was supposed to be an advantage, was removed, you were brought into that free and open market, and the energy of free trade so enlarged the buying capacity of your customers, that they were willing and able to give you, and did give you, a great deal more for your meat, your wool, and your products in general, than you would ever have got under the system of protection. Gentlemen, if that be true—and it can not, I believe, be impeached or impugned—if that be true, I do not think I need further discuss the matter, especially when so many other matters have to be discussed.

Gentlemen, I ask you again to go with me beyond the seas. And as I wish to do full justice, I will tell you what I think to be the right principles of foreign policy.

The first thing is to foster the strength of the Empire by just legislation and economy at home, thereby producing two of the great elements of national power—namely, wealth, which is a physical element, and union and contentment, which are moral elements—and to reserve the strength of the Empire, to reserve the expenditure of that strength, for great and worthy occasions abroad. Here is my first principle of foreign policy: good government at home.

My second principle of foreign policy is this: that its aim ought to be to preserve to the nations of the world—and especially, were it but for shame, when we recollect the sacred name we bear as Christians, especially to the Christian nations of the world—the blessings of peace. That is my second principle.

My third principle is this: even, gentlemen, when you do a good thing, you may do it in so bad a way that you may entirely spoil the beneficial effect; and if we were to make ourselves the apostles of peace in the sense of conveying to the minds of other nations that we thought ourselves more entitled to an opinion on that subject than they are, or to deny their rights—well, very likely we should destroy the whole value of our doctrines. In my opinion the third sound principle is this: to strive to cultivate and maintain, aye, to the very uttermost, what is called the concert of Europe; to keep the powers of Europe in union together. And why? Because by keeping all in union together you neutralize, and fetter, and bind up the selfish aims of each. I am not here to flatter either England or any of them. They have selfish aims, as, unfortunately, we in late years have too sadly shown that we, too, have had selfish aims; but their common action is fatal to selfish aims. Common action means common objects; and the only objects for which you can unite together the powers of Europe are objects connected with the common good of them all. That, gentlemen, is my third principle of foreign policy.

My fourth principle is: that you should avoid needless and entangling engagements. You may boast about them, you may brag about them, you may say you are procuring consideration for the country. You may say that an Englishman can now hold up his head among the nations. You may say that he is now not in the hands of a Liberal ministry, who thought of nothing but pounds, shillings, and pence. But what does all this come to, gentlemen? It comes to this: that you are increasing your engagements without increasing your strength; and if you increase engagements without increasing strength, you diminish strength, you abolish strength; you really reduce the empire and do not increase it. You render it less capable of performing its duties; you render it an inheritance less precious to hand on to future generations.

My fifth principle is this, gentlemen: to acknowledge the equal rights of all nations. You may sympathize with one nation more than another. Nay, you must sympathize in certain circumstances with one nation more than another. You sympathize most with those nations, as a rule, with which you have the closest connection in language, in blood, and in religion, or whose circumstances at the time seem to give the strongest claim to sympathy. But in point of right all are equal, and you have no right to set up a system under which one of them is to be placed under moral suspicion or espionage, or to be made the constant subject of invective. If you do that, but especially if you claim for yourself a superiority, a pharisaical superiority over the whole of them, then I say you may talk about your patriotism if you please, but you are a misjudging friend of your country, and in undermining the basis of the esteem and respect of other people for your country you are in reality inflicting the severest injury upon it. I have now given you, gentlemen, five principles of foreign policy. Let me give you a sixth, and then I have done.

And that sixth is: that in my opinion foreign

policy, subject to all the limitations that I have described, the foreign policy of England should always be inspired by the love of freedom. There should be a sympathy with freedom, a desire to give it scope, founded not upon visionary ideas, but upon the long experience of many generations within the shores of this happy isle, that in freedom you lay the firmest foundations both of loyalty and order; the firmest foundations for the development of individual character, and the best provision for the happiness of the nation at large. In the foreign policy of this country the name of Canning ever will be honored. The name of Russell[1] ever will be honored. The name of Palmerston ever will be honored by those who recollect the erection of the kingdom of Belgium, and the union of the disjoined provinces of Italy. It is that sympathy, not a sympathy with disorder, but, on the contrary, founded upon the deepest and most profound love of order—it is that sympathy which in my opinion ought to be the very atmosphere in which a foreign secretary of England ought to live and to move.

I make it one of my charges against the foreign policy of her majesty's government, that while they have completely estranged from this country—let us not conceal the fact—the feelings of a nation of eighty millions, for that is the number of the subjects of the Russian Empire—while they have contrived completely to

[1] Lord John Russell, afterward Earl Russell.

estrange the feelings of that nation, they have aggrandized the power of Russia. They have aggrandized the power of Russia in two ways, which I will state with perfect distinctness. They have augmented her territory. Before the European powers met at Berlin[1] Lord Salisbury met with Count Schouvaloff, and Lord Salisbury agreed that, unless he could convince Russia by his arguments in the open Congress of Berlin, he would support the restoration to the despotic power of Russia of that country north of the Danube which at the moment constituted a portion of the free State of Roumania. Why, gentlemen, what had been done by the Liberal government, which forsooth, attended to nothing but pounds, shillings, and pence? The Liberal government had driven Russia back from the Danube. Russia, which was a Danubian power before the Crimean War, lost this position on the Danube by the Crimean War; and the Tory government, which has been incensing and inflaming you against Russia, yet nevertheless, by binding itself beforehand to support, when the judgment was taken, the restoration of that country to Russia, has aggrandized the power of Russia.

It further aggrandized the power of Russia in Armenia; but I would not dwell upon that matter if it were not for a very strange circumstance. You know that an Armenian province

[1] To formulate into a treaty the results of the Russo-Turkish War of 1877-78.

was given to Russia after the war, but about that I own to you I have very much less feeling of objection. I have objected from the first, vehemently, and in every form, to the granting of territory on the Danube to Russia, and carrying back the population of a certain country from a free state to a despotic state; but with regard to the transfer of a certain portion of the Armenian people from the government of Turkey to the government of Russia, I must own that I contemplate that transfer with much greater equanimity. I have no fear myself of the territorial extensions of Russia in Asia, no fear of them whatever. I think the fears are no better than old women's fears. And I do not wish to encourage her aggressive tendencies in Asia, or anywhere else. But I admit it may be, and probably is, the case that there is some benefit attending upon the transfer of a portion of Armenia from Turkey to Russia.

With respect to Russia, I take two views of the position of Russia. The position of Russia in Central Asia I believe to be one that has, in the main, been forced upon her against her will. She has been compelled—and this is the impartial opinion of the world—she has been compelled to extend her frontier southward in Central Asia by the causes in some degree analogous to, but certainly more stringent and imperative than, the causes which have commonly led us to extend, in a far more important manner, our frontier in India; and I think it, gentlemen, much to the credit of the late government, much to the honor of Lord Clarendon and Lord Granville, that, when we were in office, we made a covenant with Russia, in which Russia bound herself to exercise no influence or interference whatever in Afghanistan, we, on the other hand, making known our desire that Afghanistan should continue free and independent. Both the powers acted with uniform strictness and fidelity upon this engagement until the day when we were removed from office. But Russia, gentlemen, has another position— her position in respect to Turkey; and here it is that I have complained of the government for aggrandizing the power of Russia; it is on this point that I most complain.

Gentlemen, the prime minister[1] speaking out, —I do not question for a moment his own sincere opinion—has made what I think one of the most unhappy and ominous allusions ever made by a minister of this country. He quoted certain words, easily rendered as "empire and liberty"—words (he said) of a Roman statesman, words descriptive of the State of Rome— and he quoted them as words which were capable of legitimate application to the position and circumstances of England. I join issue with the prime minister upon that subject, and I affirm that nothing can be more fundamentally

[1] Lord Beaconsfield.

unsound, more practically ruinous, than the establishment of Roman analogies for the guidance of British policy. What, gentlemen, was Rome? Rome was indeed an imperial State, you may tell me—I know not, I can not read the counsels of Providence—a State having a mission to subdue the world, but a State whose very basis it was to deny the equal rights, to proscribe the independent existence of other nations. That, gentlemen, was the Roman idea. It has been partially and not ill described in three lines of a translation from Virgil by our great poet Dryden, which runs as follows:

"O Rome! 'tis thine alone with awful sway
  To rule mankind, and make the world obey,
  Disposing peace and war thine own majestic way."

We are told to fall back upon this example. No doubt the word "empire" was qualified with the word "liberty." But what did the two words "liberty" and "empire" mean in a Roman mouth? They meant simply this: "liberty for ourselves, empire over the rest of mankind."

I do not think, gentlemen, that this ministry, or any other ministry, is going to place us in the position of Rome. What I object to is the revival of the idea. I care not how feebly, I care not even how—from a philosophic or historical point of view—how ridiculous the attempt at this revival may be. I say it indicates an intention—I say it indicates a frame of mind, and the frame of mind, unfortunately, I find, has been consistent with the policy of which I have given you some illustrations—the policy of denying to others the rights that we claim ourselves.

No doubt, gentlemen, Rome may have had its work to do, and Rome did its work. But modern times have brought a different state of things. Modern times have established a sisterhood of nations, equal, independent, each of them built up under that legitimate defense which public law affords to every nation, living within its own borders, and seeking to perform its own affairs; but if one thing more than another has been detestable to Europe, it has been the appearance upon the stage from time to time of men who, even in the times of the Christian civilization, have been thought to aim at universal dominion. It was this aggressive disposition on the part of Louis XIV., king of France, that led your forefathers, gentlemen, freely to spend their blood and treasure in a cause not immediately their own, and to struggle against the method of policy which, having Paris for its center, seemed to aim at an universal monarchy.

It was the very same thing, a century and a half later, which was the charge launched, and justly launched, against Napoleon: that under his dominion France was not content even with her extended limits, but Germany, and Italy, and Spain, apparently without any limit to this pestilent and pernicious process, were to be brought under the dominion or influence of France, and national equality was to be trampled under foot, and national rights denied. For that reason, England in the struggle almost exhausted herself, greatly impoverished her people, brought upon herself, and Scotland, too, the consequences of a debt that nearly crushed their energies, and poured forth their best blood without limit, in order to resist and put down these intolerable pretensions.

Gentlemen, it is but in a pale and weak and almost despicable miniature that such ideas are now set up, but you will observe that the poison lies—that the poison and the mischief lie—in the principle and not the scale.

It is the opposite principle which, I say, has been compromised by the action of the ministry, and which I call upon you, and upon any who choose to hear my views, to vindicate when the day of our election comes; I mean the sound and the sacred principle that Christendom is formed of a band of nations who are united to one another in the bonds of right; that they are without distinction of great and small; there is an absolute equality between them—the same sacredness defends the narrow limits of Belgium as attaches to the extended frontiers of Russia, or Germany, or France. I hold that he who by act or word brings that principle into peril or disparagement, however honest his intentions may be, places himself in the position of one inflicting—I will not say intending to inflict—I ascribe nothing of the sort—but inflicting injury upon his own country, and endangering the peace and all the most fundamental interests of Christian society.

BRADLAUGH

HIS PLEA AT THE BAR OF THE HOUSE[1]
(1881)

Born in 1833, died in 1891; served in the army, 1850-53; elected to Parliament in 1880, but not allowed to take his seat because he refused to take the Parliamentary oath; several times reelected, but not allowed to sit until 1886; two years later moved and carried a bill permitting members to sit if they chose by affirming instead of taking the oath.

I HAVE again to ask the indulgence of the House while I submit to it a few words in favor of my claim to do that which the law requires me to do. I now say I would not go through any form—much as I value the right to sit in this House, much as I desire and believe that this House will accord me that right —that I did not mean to be binding upon me without mental reservation, without equivocation. I would go through no form unless it were fully and completely and thoroughly binding upon me as to what it expressed or promised.

Mine has been no easy position for the last twelve months. I have been elected by the

[1] After he had made this speech, Bradlaugh was ordered to leave the House, and on refusing to do so, was placed in custody. He was reelected in the same year (1881), and formally ejected after entering and then refusing to leave the House. Similar scenes occurred in 1882 and 1883. From Bradlaugh's "The True Story of My Parliamentary Struggle," by kind permission.

free votes of a free constituency. My return is untainted. There is no charge of bribery, no charge of corruption, nor of inducing men to come drunken to the polling-booth. I come here with a pure, untainted return—not won by accident. For thirteen long years have I fought for this right—through five contested elections, including this.[1] It is now proposed to prevent me from fulfilling the duty my constituents have forced upon me. You have force: on my side is the law.

The honorable and learned member for Plymouth [Mr., and afterward Sir, Edward Clarke] spoke the truth when he said he did not ask the House to treat the matter as a question of law; but the constituencies ask me to treat it as a question of law. I, for them, ask you to treat it as a question of law. I could understand the feeling that seems to have been manifested were I some great and powerful personage. I could understand it had I a large influence behind me. I am only one of the people, and you propose to teach them that, on a mere technical question, you will put a barrier in the way of my doing my duty which you have never put in the way of anybody else.

The question is, Has my return on the ninth day of April, 1881, anything whatever to impeach it? There is no legal disqualification involved. If there were, it could be raised by petition. The honorable member for Plymouth

---

[1] His first attempt to enter Parliament was made in 1868.

says the dignity of this House is in question.
Do you mean that I can injure the dignity of
this House?—this House which has stood unrivaled for centuries?—this House, supreme
among the assemblies of the world?—this House,
which represents the traditions of liberty? I
should not have libeled you.

How is the dignity of this House to be hurt?
If what happened before the ninth day of April
is less than a legal disqualification, it is a matter
for the judgment of the constituency and not
for you. The constituency has judged me; it
has elected me; I stand here with no legal disqualification upon me. The right of the constituency to return me is an unimpeachable
right.

I know some gentlemen make light of constituencies; yet without the constituencies you
are nothing. It is from them you derive your
whole and sole authority. The honorable and
learned member for Plymouth treats lightly
the legal question. It is dangerous to make
light of the law—dangerous, because if you are
only going to rely on your strength of force to
override the law, you give a bad lesson to men
whose morality you impeach as to what should
be their duty if emergency ever came. Always
outside the House I have advocated strenuous
obedience to the law, and it is under that law
that I claim my right.

I claim to do that which the law says I must.
Frankly, I would rather have affirmed. When

I came to the table of the House I deemed I had a legal right to do it. The courts have decided against me, and I am bound to their decision.

I have the legal right to do what I propose to do. No resolution of yours can take away that legal right.

But the force that you invoke against the law to-day may to-morrow be used against you, and the use will be justified by your example. It is a fact that I have no remedy if you rely on your force. I can only be driven into a contest, wearying even to a strong man well supported, ruinous and killing to one man standing by himself—a contest in which, if I succeed, it will be injurious to you as well as to me. Injurious to me, because I can only win by lessening your repute, which I desire to maintain. The only court I have the power of appealing to is the court of public opinion, which I have no doubt in the end will do me justice.

The honorable member for Plymouth said I had the manliness on a former occasion to make an avowal of opinions to this House. I did nothing of the kind. I have never, directly or indirectly, said one word about my opinions, and this House has no right to inquire what opinions I may hold outside its walls. The only right is that which the statute gives you; my opinions there is no right to inquire into. I shelter myself under the laws of my country. This is a political assembly, met to decide on the policy of the nation and not on the religious opinions of the citizens. While I had the honor of occupying a seat in the House, when questions were raised which touched upon religious matters I abstained from uttering one word. I did not desire to say one word which might hurt the feelings of even the most tender.

But it is said, Why not have taken the oath quietly? I did not take it then, because I thought I had the right to do something else, and I have paid the penalty. I have been plunged in litigation fostered by men who had not the courage to put themselves forward. I, a penniless man, should have been ruined if it had not been that the men in workshop, pit, and factory had enabled me to fight this battle. [An interruption.]

I am sorry that honorable members can not have patience with one pleading as I plead here. It is no light task, even if you put it on the lowest personal grounds, to risk the ambition of a life on such an issue. It is a right ambition to desire to take part in the councils of the nation if you bring no store of wisdom with you and can only learn from the great intellects that we have. What will you inquire into? The right honorable baronet would inquire into my opinions. Will you inquire into my conduct, or is it only my opinions you will try here?

The honorable member for Plymouth frankly puts it, opinions. If opinions, why not conduct? Why not examine into members' conduct when they come to the table, and see if there be no members in whose way you can put a barrier?

Are members whose conduct may be obnoxious to vote my exclusion because to them my opinions are obnoxious? As to any obnoxious views supposed to be held by me, there is no duty imposed upon me to say a word. The right honorable baronet has said there has been no word of recantation.

You have no right to ask me for any recantation. Since the ninth of April you have no right to ask me for anything. If you have a legal disqualification, petition, lay it before the judges. When you ask me to make a statement you are guilty of impertinence to me, of treason to the traditions of this House, and of impeachment of the liberties of the people. My difficulty is that those who have made the most bitter attacks upon me only made them when I was not here to deal with them.

I have fought by myself. I have fought by my own hand. I have been hindered in every way that it was possible to hinder me; and it is only by the help of the people, by the pence of toilers in mine and factory, that I am here to-day after these five struggles right through thirteen years. I have won my way with them, for I have won their hearts, and now I come to you. Will you send me back from here?

Then how? You have the right, but it is the right of force and not of law. When I am once seated on these benches, then I am under your jurisdiction. At present I am under the protection of the writ from those who sent me here. I do not want to quote what has happened before; but if there be one lesson which the House has recorded more solemnly than another, it is that there should be no interference with the judgment of a constituency in sending a man to this House against whom there is no statutory disqualification. Let me appeal to the generosity of the House as well as to its strength. It has traditions of liberty on both sides. I do not complain that members on that [the Conservative] try to keep me out. They act according to their lights, and think my poor services may be injurious to them. [Cries of "No!"] Then why not let me in? It must be either a political or a religious question.

I must apologize to the House for trespassing upon its patience. I apologize because I know how generous in its listening it has been from the time of my first speech in it till now. But I ask you now, do not plunge with me into a struggle I would shun. The law gives me no remedy if the House decides against me. Do not mock at the constituencies. If you place yourselves above the law, you leave me no course save lawless agitation instead of reasonable pleading. It is easy to begin such a strife, but none knows how it would end. I have no court, no tribunal to appeal to: you have the strength of your votes at the moment. You think I am an obnoxious man, and that I have no one on my side. If that be so, then the more reason that this House, grand in the strength of its centuries of liberty, should have now that generosity in dealing with one who to-morrow may be forced into a struggle for public opinion against it.

CHURCHILL

HIS "TRUST THE PEOPLE" SPEECH [1]
(1884)

Born in 1849, died in 1895; entered Parliament in 1874; Secretary for
India in 1885; Chancellor of the Exchequer in 1886.

WHAT is the great and wide difference which
distinguishes the two great political parties who
endeavor to attract the support of the English
people? It has been well and wisely said—but I
do not think it can be too often repeated—that the
Tory party cling with veneration and affection
to the institutions of our country. The Radicals
regard them with aversion and distrust and will
always give multitudinous and specious reasons
for their destruction.

But can we, the Tory party, give no good con-
vincing reasons to the people for the faith which
is in us? We do not defend the Constitution
from mere sentiment for the past, or from any
infatuated superstition about divine right or
hereditary excellence. We defend the Constitution solely on the ground of its utility to the

[1] From a speech delivered at Birmingham on April 16, 1884, in aid
of the formation of workingmen's clubs to support the Conserva-
tive organization. These clubs have since become quite general in
England. By kind permission of the Right Honorable Winston
Churchill, the London *Times*, and Messrs. Longmans, Green & Co.

people. It is on the ground of utility alone that we go forth to meet our foes, and if we fail to make good our ground with utilitarian arguments and for utilitarian ends, then let the present combination of Throne, Lords, and Commons be for ever swept away. An hereditary throne is the surest device which has ever been imagined or invented for the perpetuation of civil order and for that first necessity of civilized society— continuity of government.

And he would be a bold man in argument who would assert that the hereditary character of the British throne is a vice, or even a defect. When we remember that the English monarchy has endured for upwards of a thousand years, what device of the wisest philosopher or the most acute mathematician could have discovered a monarch more perfect for all the purposes of a monarchy than the one whom an hereditary descent of a thousand years has provided for us? To those —and there are, I believe, many—in this town who glibly tell you that the monarchy is too expensive and is not worth the price—to them I reply that it would be impossible to devise a form of government as effectual, and yet cheaper and more simple; and that if, in an evil hour, you were to listen to those silly tattlers, the sums of money that you would ultimately have to pay for police and military in times of administrative change, the fluctuations of credit, the displacement of capital, the loss to the interests of industry and labor which constant and inevitable administrative changes would produce, and the destruction to property which, in the absence of any recognised center of authority, those administrative changes would at times occasion, instead of being counted by the few hundred thousands which are the cost price of an hereditary throne, would be counted by millions and millions. So much for the first estate of the realm which the Radical party gloomily threaten and darkly scowl at. It is as well to remind ourselves from time to time of its history, its nature, and its use.

The more immediate object of Radical detestation is the House of Lords, in which they pretend to discover all the most execrable forms of class prejudice and privilege: and I have no doubt that much of the enthusiasm with which the Radical party clamor for the Reform Bill is due to the hope which they entertain that the passage of that Bill may possibly provoke a conflict between the Lords and the Commons, in which the Lords must for ever go down. I am not concerned, nor need you be concerned, to defend all the actions of the House of Lords in modern times; but I could, if I liked, point to many bright instances of statesmanship and liberality on their part. The House of Lords makes mistakes at times, I have no doubt; but even in this respect they will compare very favorably with Mr. Gladstone's government, or even with the Radical party. I maintain that the House of Lords should be preserved solely on the ground of its utility to the people. I do not put forward as an argument for its preservation its long history, in order to show you that it possesses great merit as an institution. I do not argue, as some do, that it has acquired stability from the circumstance that by its composition it is rooted in the soil. I content myself with the fact of its existence at the present moment, and I find in it not only a powerful check on popular impulses arising from imperfect information, not only an aggregation of political wisdom and experience such as no other country can produce, but, above all, because I find in it literally the only effectual barrier against that most fatal foe to freedom, the one-man power—that power which has more than once prostrated and enslaved the liberties of France, and which constantly gives anxiety to the citizens of the United States.

From a national and imperial point of view, you need never be alarmed at the dangers of one-man power so long as the House of Lords endures. Be he minister, be he capitalist, be he demagog—be he Mr. Gladstone, or Mr. Chamberlain, or even Mr. Schnadhorst—against that bulwark of popular liberty and civil order he will dash himself in vain. The House of Lords may, perhaps, move slowly; they may, perhaps, be overcautious about accepting the merits of the legislation of the House of Commons; they may, perhaps, at times regard with some exaggeration of sentiment the extreme rights of property. That is the price you have to pay—and a

small price it is for so valuable a possession—
which guards you against so great a danger.
They are essentially of the people. Year by
year they are recruited from the people. Every
privilege, every franchise, every liberty which
is gained by the people, is treasured up and
guarded by those who, animated by tradition
and custom, by long descent and lofty name,
fear neither monarchs, nor ministers, nor men,
but only the people, whose trustees they are.
It is recorded of the Sultan Saladin that he always had a shroud carried before him in State
procession, to remind him of the perils and the
destiny of monarchs. In like manner I would
advise the English people, when speculating on
or deciding political questions, to bear always
before their minds this great constitutional fabric of the House of Lords, and to be continually
questioning and inquiring the reasons for its
existence and preservation, in order that they
may be perpetually reminded of the dangers to
which democracies are prone.

I can not pass from this subject of the House
of Lords without alluding to the other bugbear
of the Radical party, the Church of England,
and its connection with the State. This question
will be more or less directly before you at the
next election. Again I adhere to my utilitarian
line of defense, and I would urge upon you not
to lend yourselves too hastily to any project for
the demolition of the Established Church. But
I would also, in dealing with this question, min-

gle a little of the wine of sentiment with the cold
clear spring water of utilitarianism. I see in the
Church of England an immense and omnipres-
ent ramification of machinery working without
cost to the people—and daily and hourly lifting
the masses of the people, rich and poor alike,
from the dead and dreary level of the lowest and
most material cares of life, up to the comfortable
contemplation of higher and serener forms of
existence and of destiny. I see in the Church
of England a center, and a source, and a guide
of charitable effort, mitigating by its mendi-
cant importunity the violence of human misery,
whether mental or physical, and contributing
to the work of alleviation from its own not
superfluous resources; and I urge upon you not
to throw that source of charity upon the hap-
hazard almsgiving of a busy and a selfish world.

I view the Church of England eagerly co-
operating in the work of national education, not
only benefiting your children but saving your
pockets; and I remember that it has been the
work of the Church to pour forth floods of
knowledge, purely secular and scientific, even
from the days when knowledge was not; and I
warn you against hindering the diffusion of
knowledge, inspired by religion, among those
who will have devolved upon them the responsibility for the government of this wide empire.
But I own that my chief reason for supporting
the Church of England I find in the fact that,
when compared with other creeds and other

sects, it is essentially the Church of religious liberty. Whether in one direction or another, it is continually possessed by the ambition, not of excluding, but of including, all shades of religious thought, all sorts and conditions of men; and, standing out like a lighthouse over a stormy ocean, it marks the entrance to a port where the millions and the masses of those who are wearied at times with the woes of the world, and troubled often by the trials of existence, may search for and may find that peace which passeth all understanding. I can not, and will not, allow myself to believe that the English people, who are not only naturally religious, but also eminently practical, will ever consent, for the petty purpose of gratifying sectarian animosity, or for the wretched object of pandering to infidel proclivities—will ever consent to deprive themselves of so abundant a fountain of aid and consolation, or acquiesce in the demolition of an institution which elevates the life of the nation, and consecrates the acts of the State.

Last, but not least—no, rather first—in the scheme of Tory politics come the Commons of England, with their marvelous history; their ancient descent, combining the blood of many nations; their unequaled liberties, and, I believe, their splendid future. The social progress of the Commons by means of legislative reform under the lines and carried on under the protection of the institutions whose utility I have endeavored to describe to you—that must be the policy of the Tory party. Their industries must be stimulated and protected by lightening the taxation, and by a large redistribution of the incidence of taxation. Their efforts to emancipate their brethren from the vices of an undeveloped civilization—such as intemperance, crime, and a weak standard of morality—must be provoked, encouraged, and facilitated. No class interests should be allowed to stand in the way of this mighty movement, and with this movement the Tory party not only sympathize, but identify themselves.

Social reform, producing direct and immediate benefit to the Commons—that must be our cry, as opposed to the Radicals, who foolishly scream for organic change, and waste their energies and their time in attacking institutions whose destruction would not only endanger popular freedom, but would leave the social condition of the people precisely where it was before. Apply this test to every legislative proposal, to every political movement, to every combination of circumstances and phenomena, and you will know what course to take and what line of action to adopt. I was much struck the other day in the House of Commons by a sentence which fell from the prime minister, when, leaning over the table and addressing directly the Tory party, he said to them, "Trust the people."

I have long tried to make that my motto; but I know, and will not conceal, that there are still a few in our party who have that lesson yet to learn, and who have yet to understand that the Tory party of to-day is no longer identified with that small and narrow class which is connected with the ownership of land, but that its great strength can be found, and must be developed, in our large towns as well as in our country districts. Yes, trust the people. You, who are ambitious, and rightly ambitious, of being the guardians of the British Constitution, trust the people, and they will trust you—and they will follow you and join you in the defense of that Constitution against any and every foe.

I have no fear of democracy. I do not fear for minorities; I do not care for those checks and securities which Mr. Goschen seems to think of such importance. Modern checks and securities are not worth a brass farthing. Give me a fair arrangement of the constituencies, and one part of England will correct and balance the other. I do not think that electoral reform is a matter of national emergency. I should have been glad to see Parliament devote its attention and time to other matters, such as finance, local taxation, commerce, Ireland and Egypt. But I think that electoral reform is a matter of ministerial urgency, of party urgency, and that it is being treated as a question of party tactics for the purpose of uniting and stimulating the shattered Liberal majority; and it was for these reasons that I voted against the Reform Bill. But you may be sure that the English Constitution will endure and thrive, whether you add two millions of electors or two hundred to the electoral roll, so long as the Tory party are true to their past, mindful of their history, faithful to the policy which was bequeathed to them by Lord Beaconsfield. The future of the Constitution, the destinies of the Empire, are in the hands of the Tory party; and if only the leaders of the party in Parliament will have the courage of their convictions, grasp their responsibilities, and adapt their policy to those responsibilities, and if they are supported and stimulated by you who are here to-night, and by others like you in our large towns, that future and those destinies are great and assured. To rally the people round the throne, to unite the throne with the people— a loyal throne and a patriotic people—that is our policy and that is our faith.

SALISBURY

ON THE DESERTION OF GORDON IN EGYPT[1]

(1885)

Born in 1830, died in 1903; succeeded to the title of Marquis in 1868; graduated from Oxford in 1850; entered Parliament in 1854; Secretary for India in 1866; Chancellor of the University of Oxford in 1869; Secretary for India in 1874; Foreign Secretary in 1878; at the Congress of Berlin in 1878; Prime Minister during four terms—1885, 1886, 1895, 1900.

THE motion which I have the honor to lay before your lordships has a double aspect—it passes judgment on the past, and expresses an opinion with regard to the policy of the future. Some people receive with considerable impatience the idea that, at the present crisis of our country's destiny, we should examine into the past, and spend our time in judging of that which can not be recalled.

But I think that such objections are unreasonable. We depend in one of the greatest crises through which our country has ever passed on the wisdom and decision of those who guide our counsels, and we can only judge of what

[1] Delivered in the House of Lords, July 26, 1885, in support of a motion of censure on the Gladstone government. Abridged. By kind permission of the London *Times* and Messrs. Dent & Co., London.

dependence is rightly to be placed by examining their conduct in the past, and seeing whether what they have done justifies us in continuing that confidence in the difficulties which are to come.

Now, whatever else may be said of the conduct of her majesty's government, I think those who examine it carefully will find that it follows a certain rule and system, and that in that sense, if in no other, it is consistent. Their conduct at the beginning of the Egyptian affair has been analogous to their conduct at the end; throughout there has been an unwillingness to come to any requisite decision till the last moment.

There has been an absolute terror of fixing upon any settled course, and the result has been that, when the time came that external pressure forced a decision on some definite course, the moment for satisfactory action had already passed, and the measures that were taken were taken in haste, with little preparation, and often with little fitness for the emergencies with which they had to cope. The conduct of the government has been an alternation of periods of slumber and periods of rush. The rush, however vehement, has been too unprepared and too unintelligent to repair the damage which the period of slumber has effected.

Now, my lords, these three things—the case of the bombardment of Alexandria, the abandonment of the Sudan, and the mission of General Graham's force—they are all on the same plan, and they all show that remarkable characteristic of torpor during the time that action was needed, and of impulsive, hasty, and ill-considered action when the moment for action had passed by.

Their future conduct was modeled on their conduct in the past. So far was it modeled that we were able to put it to the test which establishes a scientific law. The proof of scientific law is when you can prophesy from previous experience what will happen in the future. It is exactly what took place in the present instance. We had had these three instances of the mode of working of her majesty's government before us. We knew the laws that guided their action, as astronomers, observing the motions of a comet, can discover by their observations the future path which that comet is to travel; and we prophesied what would happen in the case of General Gordon.[1]

At all events, this is clear: that throughout those six months the government knew perfectly well the danger in which General Gordon was placed. It has been said that General Gordon did not ask for troops. Well, I am surprised at that defense. One of the characteristics of General Gordon was the extreme abnegation of his nature. It was not to be expected that he should send home a telegram to say, "I am

[1] Gordon was besieged at Khartum on March 12, 1884, and was killed at the storming of the city on January 26, 1885—that is, six months previous to the date of this speech.

in great danger, therefore send me troops.'' He would probably have cut off his right hand before he would have sent such a telegram. But he did send a telegram that the people of Khartum were in danger, and that the Mahdi must win unless military succor was sent forward, and distinctly telling the government—and this is the main point—that unless they would consent to his views the supremacy of the Mahdi was assured.

My lords, is it conceivable that after that—two months after that—in May, the prime minister should have said that the government was waiting to have reasonable proof that Gordon was in danger? By that time Khartum was surrounded, and the governor of Berber had announced that his case was desperate, which was too surely proved by the massacre which took place in June.

And yet in May Mr. Gladstone was waiting for reasonable proof that they were in danger. Apparently he did not get that proof till August.

A general sent forward on a dangerous expedition does not like to go whining for assistance, unless he is pressed by absolute peril. All those great qualities which go to make men heroes are such as are absolutely incompatible with such a course, and lead them to shrink as from a great disgrace from any unnecessary appeal for exertion for their protection. It was the business of the government not to interpret General Gordon's telegrams as if they had been statutory declarations, but to judge for themselves of the circumstances of the case, and to see that those who were surrounded, who were the only three Englishmen among this vast body of Mohammedans, who were already cut off from all communication with the civilized world by the occupation of every important town upon the river, were in real danger.

I do not know any other instance in which a man has been sent to maintain such a position without a certain number of British troops. If the British troops had been there treachery would have been impossible; but sending Gordon by himself to rely on the fidelity of Africans and Egyptians was an act of extreme rashness, and if the government succeed in proving, which I do not think they can, that treachery was inevitable, they only pile up an additional reason for their condemnation. I confess it is very difficult to separate this question from the personal matters involved. It is very difficult to argue it on purely abstract grounds without turning for a moment to the character of the man who was engaged and the terrible position in which he was placed.

When we consider all that he underwent, all that he sacrificed in order to serve the government in a moment of extreme exigency, there is something infinitely pathetic in reflecting on his feelings, as day after day, week after week, month after month passed by—as he spared no exertions, no personal sacrifice, to perform the duties that were placed upon him—as he lengthened out the siege by inconceivable prodigies of ingenuity, of activity, of resource—and as, in spite of it all, in spite of the deep devotion to his country, which had prompted him to this great risk and undertaking, the conviction gradually grew upon him that his country had abandoned him.

It is terrible to think what he must have suffered when at last, as a desperate measure to save those he loved, he parted with the only two Englishmen with whom during those long months he had any converse, and sent Stewart and Power down the river to escape from the fate which had become inevitable to himself. It is very painful to think of the reproaches to his country and to his country's government that must have passed through the mind of that devoted man during those months of unmerited desertion. In Gordon's letter of the fourteenth of December he said: "All is up. I expect a catastrophe in ten days' time; it would not have been so if our people had kept me better informed as to their intentions."

They had no intentions to inform him of. They were merely acting from hand to mouth to avert the parliamentary censure with which they were threatened. They had no plan, they had no intentions to carry out. If they could have known their intentions, a great hero would have been saved to the British army, a great disgrace would not have fallen on the English government.

Now, by the light of this sad history, what are the prospects for the future? Was there ever a time when clearness of plan and distinctness of policy were more required than they are now? I am not going to say that the policy of the government is bad. It would be paying them an extravagant compliment if I said so. They have no policy.

On one point only do they put down their foot and that is, the Egyptians shall not keep the Sudan. We were told that they were going to smash the Mahdi, but now we are to make peace with the smashed Mahdi. If you smash the Mahdi thoroughly he will be of no use to you, and if you do not smash him thoroughly he may maintain at the bottom of his heart a certain resentment against the process of being smashed.

Now, let us examine what are the interests of England in this matter. With Mediterranean politics as such we have no great interest to concern ourselves; but Egypt stands in a peculiar position. It is the road to India. The condition of Egypt can never be indifferent to us, and, more than that, we have a duty to insist —that our influence shall be predominant there. I do not care by what technical arrangements that result is to be obtained; but, with all due regard to the rights of the suzerain, the influence of England in Egypt must be supreme.

Now, the influence of England in Egypt is threatened from two sides. It is threatened from the north diplomatically. I do not think it is necessary that the powers should have taken up the position they have done, and I believe that with decent steering it might have been avoided; but, unfortunately, we have to face inchoate schemes which will demand the utmost jealousy and vigilance of Parliament. I do not know what arrangement the government has arrived at, but I greatly fear that it may include a multiple control, and to that I believe this country will be persistently and resolutely hostile.

But we have to face a danger of another kind. We have forces of fanatical barbarians let loose upon the south of Egypt, and owing to the blunders that have been committed this danger has reached a terrible height. Unless we intend to give over Egypt to barbarism and anarchy we must contrive to check this inroad of barbarian fanaticism, which is personified in the character and action of the Mahdi. General Gordon never said a truer thing than that you do this by simply drawing a military line. If the insurgent Mohammedans reach the north of Egypt it will not be so much by their military force, as by the moral power of their example. We have therefore to check this advance of the Mahdi's power.

Her majesty's government in the glimpses of policy which they occasionally afford us have alluded to the possibility of setting up a good government in the Sudan. I quite agree that a good government is essential to us in the Sudan. It is the only dyke we can really erect to keep out this inundation of barbarism and fanatical forces.

All those advantages can be obtained if England will lay down a definite policy and will adhere to it, but consistency of policy is absolutely necessary. We have to assure our friends that we shall stand by them; we have to assure our enemies that we are permanently to be feared. The blunders of the last three years have placed us in the presence of terrible problems and difficulties. We have great sacrifices to make. This railway will be an enormous benefit to Africa, but do not let us conceal from ourselves that it is a task of no small magnitude. If you are to carry this railway forward you will not only have to smash the Mahdi, but Osman Digna also.

All this will involve great sacrifices and the expenditure not only of much money, but of more of the English blood of which the noblest has already been poured forth. And we are not so strong as we were. At first all nations sympathized with us, but now they look on us coldly and even with hostility. Those who were our friends have become indifferent, those who were indifferent have become our adversaries; and if our misfortunes and disasters go on much longer we shall have Europe saying that they can not trust us, that we are too weak, that our prestige is too low to justify us in undertaking this task.

My lords, those great dangers can only be faced by a consistent policy, which can only be conducted by a ministry capable of unity of counsel and decision of purpose. I have shown you that from this ministry we can expect no such results. They can only produce after their kind. They will only do what they have already done. You can not look for unity of counsel from an administration that is hopelessly divided. You can not expect a resolute policy from those whose purpose is hopelessly halting.

It is for this reason, my lords, that I ask you to record your opinion that from a ministry in whom the first of all—the quality of decision of purpose—is wanting, you can hope no good in this crisis of our country's fate. And if you continue to trust them, if for any party reasons Parliament continues to abandon to their care the affairs which they have hitherto so hopelessly mismanaged, you must expect to go on from bad to worse; you must expect to lose the little prestige which you retain; you must expect to find in other portions of the world the results of the lower consideration that you occupy in the eyes of mankind; you must expect to be drawn on, degree by degree, step by step, under the cover of plausible excuses, under the cover of highly philanthropic sentiments, to irreparable disasters, and to disgrace that it will be impossible to efface.

SPURGEON

MEN MADE RICH BY THE POVERTY OF CHRIST [1]

Born in 1834, died in 1892; Pastor of a church near Cambridge in 1851; Pastor in London in 1853; removed to the new Tabernacle in 1861; founder of a pastors' college as well as of schools, alms-houses, and an orphan asylum.

THINK not that our Savior began to live when he was born of the Virgin Mary; imagine not that he dates his existence from the manger at Bethlehem; remember he is the Eternal, he is before all things, and by him all things consist. There was never a time in which there was not God. And just so there was never a period in which there was not Christ Jesus our Lord. He is self-existent, has no beginning of days, neither end of years; he is the immortal, invisible, the only wise God, our Savior. Now, in the past eternity which had elapsed before his mission to this world, we are told that Jesus Christ was rich; and to those of us who believe his glories and trust in his divinity it is not hard to see how he was so. Jesus was rich in possessions. Lift up thine eye, believer, and for a moment review the riches of my Lord

[1] From a sermon sometimes known under the title of "The Condescension of Christ."

Jesus before he condescended to become poor for thee. Behold him sitting upon his throne and declaring his own all-sufficiency. "If I were hungry, I would not tell thee, for the cattle on a thousand hills are mine. Mine are the hidden treasures of gold; mine are the pearls that the diver can not reach; mine every precious thing that earth has seen."

But he had, besides, that which makes men richer still. We have heard of kings in olden times who were fabulously rich, and when their riches were summed up we read in the old romances, "And this man was possessed of the philosopher's stone, whereby he turned all things into gold." Surely all the treasures that he had before were as nothing compared with this precious stone that brought up the rear. Now, whatever might be the wealth of Christ in things created, he had the power of creation, and therein lay his boundless wealth. If he had pleased he could have spoken worlds into existence; he had but to lift his finger, and a new universe as boundless as the present would have leaped into existence. At the will of his mind millions of angels would have stood before him, legions of bright spirits would have flashed into being. He spake, and it was done; he commanded, and it stood fast. He who said, "Light be," and light was, had power to say to all things, "Be," and they should "be." Herein, lay his riches; this creating power was one of the brightest jewels of his crown.

We call men rich, too, who have honor, and tho men have never so much wealth, yet if they be in disgrace and shame they must not reckon themselves among the rich. But our Lord Jesus had honor, honor such as none but a divine being could receive. When he sat upon his throne, before he relinquished the glorious mantle of his sovereignty to become a man, all earth was filled with his glory. He could look both beneath and all around him, and the inscription, "Glory be unto God," was written over all space; day and night the smoking incense of praise ascended before him from golden vials held by spirits who bowed in reverence; the harps of myriads of cherubim and seraphim continually thrilled with his praise, and the voices of all those mighty hosts were ever eloquent in adoration.

It may be that on set days the princes from the far-off realms, the kings, the mighty ones of his boundless realms, came to the court of Christ and brought each his annual revenue. Oh! who can tell but that in the vast eternity, at certain grand eras, the great bell was rung, and all the mighty hosts that were created gathered together in solemn review before his throne? Who can tell the high holiday that was kept in the court of heaven when these bright spirits bowed before his throne in joy and gladness, and, all united, raised their voices in shouts and hallelujahs such as mortal ear has never heard?

Oh! can ye tell the depths of the rivers of praise that flowed hard by the city of God? Can ye imagine to yourselves the sweetness of that harmony that perpetually poured into the ear of Jesus, Messiah, King, Eternal, equal with God his Father? No; at the thought of the glory of his kingdom, and the riches and majesty of his power, our souls are spent within us; our words fail; we can not utter the tithe of his glories.

Nor was he poor in any other sense. He that hath wealth on earth, and honor, too, is poor if he hath not love. I would rather be the pauper, dependent upon charity, and have love, than I would be the prince, despised and hated, whose death is looked for as a boon. Without love man is poor—give him all the diamonds, and pearls, and gold that mortal hath conceived.

But Jesus was not poor in love. When he came to earth, he did not come to get our love because his soul was solitary. Oh, no, his Father hath a full delight in him from all eternity! The heart of Jehovah, the first person of the Sacred Trinity, was divinely, immutably linked to him; he was beloved of the Father and of the Holy Spirit; the three persons took a sacred complacency and delight in each other. And besides that, how was he loved by those bright spirits who had not fallen! I can not tell what countless orders and creatures there are created who still stand fast in obedience to God. It is not possible for us to know whether there are, or not, as many races of created beings as we know there are created men on earth.

We can not tell but that in the boundless regions of space there are worlds inhabited by beings infinitely superior to us; but certain it is, there were the holy angels, and they loved our Savior; they stood day and night with wings outstretched, waiting for his commands, hearkening to the voice of his word; and when he bade them fly there was love in their countenance and joy in their hearts.

They loved to serve him, and it is not all fiction that when there was war in heaven, and when God cast out the devil and his legions, then the elect angels showed their love to him, being valiant in fight and strong in power. He wanted not our love to make him happy; he was rich enough in love without us.

What! was it true that he whose crown was all bedight with stars would lay that crown aside? What! was it certain that he about whose shoulders was cast the purple of the universe would become a man dressed in a peasant's garment? Could it be true that he who was everlasting and immortal would one day be nailed to a cross? Oh, how their wonderment increased! They desired to look into it. And when he descended from on high they followed him; for Jesus was "seen of angels," and seen in a special sense, for they looked upon him in rapturous amazement, wondering what it all could mean. "He for our sakes became poor."

And now wonder, ye angels, the Infinite has become an infant; he, upon whose shoulders the universe does hang, hangs at his mother's breast; he who created all things and bears up the pillars of creation hath now become so weak that he must be carried by a woman! And oh, wonder, ye that knew him in his riches, while ye admire his poverty!

Where sleeps the new-born King? Had he the best room in Cæsar's palace? Hath a cradle of gold been prepared for him, and pillows of down on which to rest his head? No; where the ox fed, in the dilapidated stable, in the manger, there the Savior lies, swathed in the swaddling-bands of the children of poverty! Nor there doth he rest long; on a sudden mother must carry him to Egypt; he goeth there and becometh a stranger in a strange land. When he comes back, see him that made the worlds handle the hammer and the nails, assisting his father in the trade of a carpenter!

Never was there a poorer man than Christ; he was the prince of poverty. He was the reverse of Crœsus—he might be on top of the hill of riches, Christ stood in the lowest vale of poverty. Look at his dress; it is woven from the top throughout, the garment of the poor! As for his food, he oftentimes did hunger and always was dependent upon the charity of others for the relief of his wants! He who scattered the harvest o'er the broad acres of the world had not sometimes wherewithal to stay the pangs of hunger! He who digged the springs of the ocean sat upon a well and said to a Samaritan woman, ''Give me to drink!''

He rode in no chariot, he walked his weary way, footsore, o'er the flints of Galilee! He had not where to lay his head. He looked upon the fox as it hurried to its burrow, and the fowl as it went to its resting place, and he said, ''Foxes have holes, and the birds of the air have nests; but I, the Son of man, have not where to lay my head.''

He who had once been waited on by angels becomes the servant of servants, takes a towel, girds himself, and washes his disciples' feet! He who was once honored with the hallelujahs of ages is now spit upon and despised! He who was loved by his Father and had abundance of the wealth of affection could say, ''He that eateth bread with me hath lifted up his heel against me.''

Follow him along his *via dolorosa* until at last you meet him among the olives of Gethsemane; see him sweating great drops of blood! Follow him to the pavement of Gabbatha; see him pouring out rivers of gore beneath the cruel whips of Roman soldiers! With weeping eye follow him to the cross of Calvary, see him nailed there! Mark his poverty, so poor that they have stripped him naked from head to foot and exposed him to the face of the sun! So poor that when he asked them for water they gave him vinegar to drink! So poor that his unpillowed head is girt with thorns in death!

Methinks, when he was tempted of the devil in the wilderness, it must have been hard in him to have restrained himself from dashing the devil into pieces. If I had been the Son of God, methinks, feeling as I do now, if that devil had tempted me, I should have dashed him into the nethermost hell in the twinkling of an eye! And then conceive the patience our Lord must have had, standing on the pinnacle of the temple, when the devil said, "Fall down and worship me." He would not touch him, the vile deceiver, but let him do what he pleased. Oh! what might of misery and love there must have been in the Savior's heart when he was spit upon by the men he had created; when the eyes he himself had filled with vision looked on him with scorn, and when the tongues to which he himself had given utterance hissed and blasphemed him!

The reason why Christ died was "that we through his poverty might be rich." He became poor from his riches, that our poverty might become rich out of his poverty. Brethren, we have now a joyful theme before us: those who are partakers of the Savior's blood are rich. All those for whom the Savior died, having believed in his name and given themselves to him, are this day rich. And yet I have some of you here who can not call a foot of land your own. You have nothing to call your own to-day; you know not how you will be supported through another week; you are poor, and yet if you be a child of God I do know that Christ's end is answered in you; you are rich. No, I did not mock you when I said you were rich: I did not taunt you—you are. You are really rich; you are rich in his possessions; you have in your possession now things more costly than gems, more valuable than gold and silver.

Ah, Egypt, thou wert rich when thy granaries were full, but those granaries might be emptied; Israel was far richer when they could not see their granaries, but only saw the manna drop from heaven day by day. Now, Christian, that is thy portion—the portion of the fountain always flowing, and not of the cisternful, and soon to be emptied.

But remember, O saint, that thy wealth does not all lie in thy possession just now; remember thou art rich in promises. Let a man be never so poor as the metal that he hath, let him have in his possession promissory notes from rich and true men, and he says, ''I have no gold in my purse, but here is a note for such and such a sum—I know the signature—I can trust the firm—I am rich, tho I have no metal in hand.''

And now, Christian, in heaven there is a crown of gold which is thine to-day; it will be no more thine when thou hast it on thy head than it is now.

I remember to have heard it reported that I once spoke in metaphor, and bade Christians

look at all the crowns hanging in rows in heaven
—very likely I did say it, but if not, I will
say it now. Up, Christian, see the crowns all
ready, and mark thine own; stand thou and
wonder at it; see with what pearls it is bedight, and how heavy it is with gold! And
that is for thy head, thy poor aching head;
thy poor tortured brain shall yet have that crown
for its arraying!

And see that garment, it is stiff with gems,
and white like snow; and that is for thee! When
thy week-day garment shall be done with, this
shall be the raiment of thy everlasting Sabbath.
When thou hast worn out this poor body there
remaineth for thee "a house not made with
hands, eternal in the heavens."

Up to the summit, Christian, and survey thine
inheritance; and when thou hast surveyed it all,
when thou hast seen thy present possessions, thy
promised possessions, thine entailed possessions,
then remember that all these were bought by
the poverty of thy Savior! Look thou upon
all thou hast and say, "Christ bought them for
me." Look thou on every promise and see the
bloodstains on it; yea, look, too, on the harps
and crowns of heaven and read the bloody purchase! Remember, thou couldst never have
been anything but a damned sinner unless Christ
had bought thee! Remember, if he had remained in heaven thou wouldst for ever have
remained in hell; unless he had shrouded and
eclipsed his own honor thou wouldst never have
had a ray of light to shine upon thee.

Therefore bless his dear name, extol him, trace every stream to the fountain; and bless him who is the source and the fountain of everything thou hast. Brethren, "Ye know the grace of our Lord Jesus Christ, that, tho he was rich, yet for your sakes he became poor, that ye through his poverty might be rich."

Remember, Christ came to make those rich that have nothing of their own. My Savior is a physician; if you can heal yourself he will have nothing to do with you. Remember, my Savior came to clothe the naked. He will clothe you if you have not a rag of your own; but unless you let him do it from head to foot he will have nothing to do with you. Christ says he will never have a partner; he will do all or none. Come, then, hast thou given up all to Christ? Hast thou no reliance and trust save in the cross of Jesus? Then thou hast answered the question well. Be happy, be joyous; if death should surprise thee the next hour, thou art secure. Go on thy way and rejoice in the hope of the glory of God.

Remember, Christ will not reject thee; thou mayest reject him. Remember now, there is the cup of mercy put to thy lip by the hand of Jesus. I know, if thou feelest thy need, Satan may tempt thee not to drink, but he will not prevail; thou wilt put thy lip feebly and faintly, perhaps, to it. But oh! do but sip it; and the first draught shall give thee bliss; and the deeper thou shalt drink the more heaven shalt thou know.

Sinner, believe on Jesus Christ; hear the whole gospel preached to thee. It is written in God's Word, "He that believeth and is baptized shall be saved." Hear me translate it: He that believeth and is immersed shall be saved. Believe thou, trust thyself on the Savior, make a profession of thy faith in baptism, and then thou mayest rejoce in Jesus, that he hath saved thee. But remember not to make a profession till thou hast believed; remember, baptism is nothing until thou hast faith. Remember, it is a farce and a falsehood until thou hast first believed; and afterward it is nothing but the profession of thy faith.

BIRRELL

THE DISTINCTION OF BURKE[1]

Born in 1850; graduated from Cambridge in 1872; Barrister in 1875; Professor of Law in 1896; Member of Parliament in 1899; Member of the Cabinet in 1906.

THE first great fact to remember is, that the Edmund Burke we are all agreed in regarding as one of the proudest memories of the House of Commons was an Irishman. When we are in our next fit of political depression about that island, and are about piously to wish, as the poet Spenser tells us men were wishing even in his time, that it were not adjacent, let us do a little national stock-taking, and calculate profits as well as losses.

Burke was not only an Irishman, but a typical one—of the very kind many Englishmen, and even possibly some Scotchmen, make a point of disliking. I do not say he was an aboriginal Irishman, but his ancestors are said to have settled in the county of Galway, under Strongbow, in King Henry the Second's time, when Ireland was first conquered and our troubles began. This, at all events, is a better Irish pedigree than Mr. Parnell's.

[1] From a lecture delivered before the Edinburgh Philosophical Society. Printed here by kind permission of Mr. Birrell.

Burke was brought up in the Protestant faith of his father, and was never in any real danger of deviating from it; but I can not doubt that his regard for his Catholic fellow subjects, his fierce repudiation of the infamies of the penal code—whose horrors he did something to mitigate—his respect for antiquity, and his historic sense, were all quickened by the fact that a tenderly loved and loving mother belonged through life and in death to an ancient and an outraged faith.

Burke came to London with a cultivated curiosity, and in no spirit of desperate determination to make his fortune. That the study of the law interested him can not be doubted, for everything interested him, and particularly the stage. Like the sensible Irishman he was, he lost his heart to Peg Woffington on the first opportunity. He was fond of roaming about the country, during, it is to be hoped, vacation time only, and is to be found writing the most cheerful letters to his friends in Ireland (all of whom are persuaded that he is going some day to be somebody, tho sorely puzzled to surmise what thing or when, so pleasantly does he take life), from all sorts of out-of-the-way country places, where he lodges with quaint old landladies who wonder maternally why he never gets drunk, and generally mistake him for an author until he pays his bill.

When in town he frequented debating societies in Fleet Street and Covent Garden, and made his first speeches; for which purpose he would, unlike some debaters, devote studious hours to getting up the subjects to be discussed. There is good reason to believe that it was in this manner his attention was first directed to India. He was at all times a great talker, and, Doctor Johnson's dictum notwithstanding, a good listener. He was endlessly interested in everything—in the state of the crops, in the last play, in the details of all trades, the rhythm of all poems, the plots of all novels, and indeed in the course of every manufacture. And so for six years he went up and down, to and fro, gathering information, imparting knowledge, and preparing himself, tho he knew not for what.

But great as were Burke's literary powers, and passionate as was his fondness for letters and for literary society, he never seems to have felt that the main burden of his life lay in that direction. He looked to the public service, and this tho he always believed that the pen of a great writer was a more powerful and glorious weapon than any to be found in the armory of politics.

It is satisfactory to notice how from the very first Burke's intellectual preeminence, character, and aims were clearly admitted and most cheerfully recognized by his political and social superiors; and in the long correspondence in which he engaged with most of them, there is not a trace to be found, on one side or the other, of anything approaching to either patronage or servility. Burke advises them, exhorts them, expostulates with them, condemns their aristocratic languor, fans their feeble flames, drafts their motions, dictates their protests, visits their houses, and generally supplies them with facts, figures, poetry, and romance.

To all this they submit with much humility. The Duke of Richmond once indeed ventured to hint to Burke, with exceeding delicacy, that he (the Duke) had a small private estate to attend to as well as public affairs; but the validity of the excuse was not admitted. The part Burke played for the next fifteen years with relation to the Rockingham party reminds me of the functions I have observed performed in lazy families by a soberly clad and eminently respectable person who pays them domiciliary visits, and, having admission everywhere, goes about mysteriously from room to room, winding up all the clocks. This is what Burke did for the Rockingham party—he kept it going.

But fortunately for us, Burke was not content with private adjuration, or even public speech. His literary instincts, his dominating desire to persuade everybody that he, Edmund Burke, was absolutely in the right, and every one of his opponents hopelessly wrong, made him turn to the pamphlet as a propaganda, and in his hands—

> "The thing became a trumpet whence he blew
> Soul-animating strains."

So accustomed are we to regard Burke's pamphlets as specimens of our noblest literature, and to see them printed in comfortable volumes, that we are apt to forget that in their origin they were but the children of the pavement, the publications of the hour.

I have now rather more than kept my word so far as Burke's preparliamentary life is concerned, and will proceed to mention some of the circumstances that may serve to account for the fact, that when the Rockingham party came into power for the second time in 1782, Burke, who was their life and soul, was only rewarded with a minor office.[1]

First, then, it must be recorded sorrowfully of Burke that he was always desperately in debt, and in this country no politician under the rank of a baronet can ever safely be in debt. Burke's finances are, and always have been marvels and mysteries; but one thing must be said of them—that the malignity of his enemies, both Tory enemies and Radical enemies, has never succeeded in formulating any charge of dishonesty against him that has not been at once completely pulverized, and shown on the facts to be impossible.

Burke's purchase of the estate at Beaconsfield in 1768, only two years after he entered Parliament, consisting as it did of a good house and 1,600 acres of land, has puzzled a great

[1] Burke in this ministry was paymaster-general and privy councillor.

many good men—much more than it ever did
Edmund Burke. But how did he get the money?
After an Irish fashion—by not getting it at all.

Two-thirds of the purchase-money remained on
mortgage, and the balance he borrowed; or, as
he puts it, "With all I could collect of my own,
and by the aid of my friends, I have established
a root in the country." That is how Burke
bought Beaconsfield, where he lived till his end
came; whither he always hastened when his
sensitive mind was tortured by the thought of
how badly men governed the world; where he
entertained all sorts and conditions of men—
Quakers, Brahmins (for whose ancient rites he
provided suitable accommodation in a greenhouse), nobles and abbés flying from revolutionary France, poets, painters, and peers, no one
of whom ever long remained a stranger to his
charm.

Farming, if it is to pay, is a pursuit of small
economies; and Burke was far too Asiatic, tropical, and splendid to have anything to do with
small economies. His expenditure, like his rhetoric, was in the "grand style." He belongs to
Charles Lamb's great race, "the men who bor-
row." But indeed it was not so much that
Burke borrowed as that men lent.

Right-feeling men did not wait to be asked.
Doctor Brocklesby, that good physician, whose
name breathes like a benediction through the
pages of the biographies of the best men of his
time, who soothed Doctor Johnson's last melan-

choly hours, and for whose supposed heterodoxy
the dying man displayed so tender a solicitude,
wrote to Burke in the strain of a timid suitor
proposing for the hand of a proud heiress, to
know whether Burke would be so good as to accept 1,000*l.* at once, instead of waiting for the
writer's death.   Burke felt no hesitation in
obliging so old a friend.

Garrick, who, tho fond of money, was as
generous-hearted a fellow as ever brought down
a house, lent Burke 1,000*l.*   Sir Joshua Reyn-
olds, who had been reckoned stingy, by his will
left Burke 2,000*l.*, and forgave him another
2,000*l.* which he had lent him.   The Marquis of
Rockingham, by his will, directed all Burke's
bonds held by him to be canceled. They amounted
to 30,000*l.*   Burke's patrimonial estate was sold
by him for 4,000*l.*; and I have seen it stated that
he had received altogether from family sources
as much as 20,000*l.*

And yet he was always poor, and was glad
at the last to accept pensions from the Crown
in order that he might not leave his wife a beg-
gar.   This good lady survived her illustrious
husband twelve years, and seemed, as his widow,
to have some success in paying his bills, for at
her death all remaining demands were found to
be discharged.

Had Burke been a moralist of the caliber of
Charles James Fox, he might have amassed a
fortune large enough to keep up half a dozen
Beaconsfields, by simply doing what all his pred-

ecessors in the office he held, including Fox's own father, the truly infamous first Lord Holland, had done—namely, by retaining for his own use the interest on all balances of the public money from time to time in his hands as paymaster of the forces. But Burke carried his passion for good government into actual practise, and, cutting down the emoluments of his office to a salary (a high one, no doubt), effected a saving to the country of some 25,000l. a year, every farthing of which might have gone without remark into his own pocket.

Burke had no vices save of style and temper; nor was any of his expenditure a profligate squandering of money. It all went in giving employment or disseminating kindness. He sent the painter Barry to study art in Italy. He saved the poet Crabbe from starvation and despair, and thus secured to the country one who owns the unrivaled distinction of having been the favorite poet of the three greatest intellectual factors of the age (scientific men excepted)—Lord Byron, Sir Walter Scott, and Cardinal Newman.

Yet so distorted are men's views that the odious and antisocial excesses of Fox at the gambling-table are visited with a blame usually wreathed in smiles, whilst the financial irregularities of a noble and pure-minded man are thought fit matter for the fiercest censure or the most lordly contempt.

Next to Burke's debts, some of his companions

and intimates did him harm and injured his consequence. His brother Richard, whose brogue we are given to understand was simply appalling, was a good-for-nothing, with a dilapidated reputation. Then there was another Mr. Burke, who was no relation, but none the less was always about, and to whom it was not safe to lend money. Burke's son, too, whose death he mourned so pathetically, seems to have been a failure, and is described by a candid friend as a nauseating person. To have a decent following is important in politics.

It now only remains for me, drawing upon my stock of assurance, to essay the analysis of the essential elements of Burke's mental character, and I therefore at once proceed to say that it was Burke's peculiarity and his glory to apply the imagination of a poet of the first order to the facts and the business of life. Arnold says of Sophocles—

"He saw life steadily and saw it whole."

Substitute for the word "life" the words "organized society," and you get a peep into Burke's mind.

There was a catholicity about his gaze. He knew how the whole world lived. Everything contributed to this: his vast desultory reading; his education, neither wholly academical nor entirely professional; his long years of apprenticeship in the service of knowledge; his wanderings up and down the country; his vast conversational powers; his enormous correspondence with all sorts of people; his unfailing interest in all pursuits, trades, manufactures,—all helped to keep before him, like motes dancing in a sunbeam, the huge organism of modern society, which requires for its existence and for its development the maintenance of credit and of order.

Burke's imagination led him to look out over the whole land; the legislator devising new laws, the judge expounding and enforcing old ones, the merchant despatching his goods and extending his credit, the banker advancing the money of his customers upon the credit of the merchant, the frugal man slowly accumulating the store which is to support him in old age, the ancient institutions of Church and University with their seemly provisions for sound learning and true religion, the parson in his pulpit, the poet pondering his rhymes, the farmer eyeing his crops, the painter covering his canvases, the player educating the feelings.

Burke saw all this with the fancy of a poet, and dwelt on it with the eye of a lover. But love is the parent of fear, and none knew better than Burke how thin is the lava layer between the costly fabric of society and the volcanic heats and destroying flames of anarchy. He trembled for the fair frame of all established things, and to his horror saw men, instead of covering the thin surface with the concrete, digging in it for abstractions, and asking fundamental questions about the origin of society, and why one man should be born rich and another poor.

Burke was no prating optimist: it was his very knowledge how much could be said against society that quickened his fears for it. There is no shallower criticism than that which accuses Burke in his later years of apostasy from so-called Liberal opinions. Burke was all his life through a passionate maintainer of the established order of things, and a ferocious hater of abstractions and metaphysical politics.

The same ideas that explode like bombs through his diatribes against the French Revolution are to be found shining with a mild effulgence in the comparative calm of his earlier writings. I have often been struck with a resemblance, which I hope is not wholly fanciful, between the attitude of Burke's mind toward government and that of Cardinal Newman toward religion.

Both these great men belong, by virtue of their imaginations, to the poetic order, and they both are to be found dwelling with amazing eloquence, detail, and wealth of illustration on the varied elements of society. Both seem as they write to have one hand on the pulse of the world, and to be forever alive to the throb of its action; and Burke, as he regarded humanity swarming like bees into and out of their hives of industry, asked himself the question, How are these men to be saved from anarchy? whilst Newman puts to himself the question, How are these men to be saved from atheism? Both saw the perils of free inquiry divorced from practical affairs.

If either of these great men has been guilty of intellectual excesses, those of Burke may be attributed to his dread of anarchy, those of Newman to his dread of atheism. Neither of them was prepared to rest content with a scientific frontier, an imaginary line. So much did they dread their enemy, so alive were they to the terrible strength of some of his positions, that they could not agree to dispense with the protection afforded by the huge mountains of prejudice and the ancient rivers of custom. The sincerity of either man can only be doubted by the bigot and the fool.

But Burke, apart from his fears, had a constitutional love for old things, simply because they were old. Anything mankind had ever worshiped, or venerated, or obeyed, was dear to him. I have already referred to his providing his Brahmins with a greenhouse for the purpose of their rites, which he watched from outside with great interest. One can not fancy Cardinal Newman peeping through a window to see men worshiping false tho ancient gods. Warren Hastings's high-handed dealings with the temples and time-honored if scandalous customs of the Hindus filled Burke with horror. So, too, he respected Quakers, Presbyterians,

Independents, Baptists, and all those whom he called Constitutional Dissenters.

He has a fine passage somewhere about rust; for with all his passion for good government he dearly loved a little rust. In this phase of character he reminds one not a little of another great writer—whose death literature has still reason to deplore—George Eliot; who, in her love for old hedge-rows and barns and crumbling moss-grown walls, was a writer after Burke's own heart, whose novels he would have sat up all night to devour; for did he not deny with warmth Gibbon's statement that he had read all five volumes of "Evelina" in a day? "The thing is impossible," cried Burke; "they took me three days, doing nothing else." Now, "Evelina" is a good novel, but "Silas Marner" is a better.

Wordsworth has been called the High Priest of Nature. Burke may be called the High Priest of Order—a lover of settled ways, of justice, peace, and security. His writings are a storehouse of wisdom, not the cheap shrewdness of the mere man of the world, but the noble, animating wisdom of one who has the poet's heart as well as the statesman's brain.

Nobody is fit to govern this country who has not drunk deep at the springs of Burke. "Have you read your Burke?" is at least as sensible a question to put to a parliamentary candidate, as to ask him whether he is a total abstainer or a desperate drunkard. Something there may be about Burke to regret, and more to dispute; but that he loved justice and hated iniquity is certain, as also it is that for the most part he dwelt in the paths of purity, humanity, and good sense. May we be found adhering to them!

JAMES BRYCE

ON THE GOVERNMENT OF IRELAND BILL

(1886)

Born in 1838; practised law until 1882; Regius Professor of Civil
Law at Oxford 1870–1893; elected to Parliament in 1880; Under-Secretary of State for Foreign Affairs in 1886; President of the Board
of Trade in 1894; author of "The American Commonwealth," 1888;
Chief Secretary to the Lord-Lieutenant of Ireland in 1906.

NOTHING is more essential than that in passing
a measure like this we should base it on firm
legal grounds, and that we should clearly understand what relation the law we are asked to pass
is to bear to the political action that is to go on
under it. I do not think anything better deserves
the attention of the House, and I hope the House
will suffer me to deal somewhat minutely with it.

My right honorable and learned friend laid
down three propositions: the first was that by
this Bill the unity of the empire would be destroyed; the second, that the imperial Parliament would not be able, henceforth, to legislate
for Ireland; and the third, that the sovereignty
of the imperial Parliament would disappear.
My right honorable and learned friend said that
the unity of the empire was created by the union
of Parliament. What, was there no unity of the
British Empire before 1800? Were we not one

---

[1] From a speech in the House of Commons on May 17, 1886. By
kind permission of Mr. Bryce and Cornelius Buck & Son.

empire during that century of glory which ended in 1800, when the foundations of our Indian and Colonial dominion were laid, when so many successful wars were waged by British soldiers and sailors? Or how can it be said that there will be less unity of the empire under the Bill than there was between 1782 and 1800, when there were two crowns, two armies, and two Mutiny Acts?

My right honorable and learned friend said the union of the crown in the same person did not make a United Kingdom, and he cited the case of Hanover; but he forgot that when our sovereigns were electors of Hanover they were members of the Holy Roman Empire, and afterward, when that empire had already vanished, they became, in 1815, members of the Germanic Confederation. When he says that that which makes unity of laws is the unity of the law-making power, does he remember that in a country which has long been united, and which in every decade of its existence tends to become more and more united—I mean the United States of North America—there are thirty-eight separate legislatures which enjoy within their proper sphere supreme legislative power? These legislatures are entirely uncontrolled by the Federal Congress on certain subjects—subjects of wide compass and great consequence. Not only in the different States are the laws different, but the spirit in which these State laws are administered is also different.

The noble lord, the member for Rossendale [the Marquis of Hartington], said, on the first night of the debate, that he looked upon it as a most important thing that an Englishman should find himself at home if he traveled to Ireland; but that he could not do that if the laws of Ireland were to be not only different in themselves, but also administered by a different executive, and in a different spirit. This is exactly what happens in the United States. If a citizen travels from Massachusetts or Pennsylvania to Arkansas or Texas, he will find that the laws are different; that the executive authority is different and independent; and that the laws are administered in these newer western States in a very different and sometimes an unfortunate manner; but that does not prevent citizens of the United States who travel out of one State into another from feeling themselves everywhere at home.

The second argument of my right honorable and learned friend was that under the Bill the imperial Parliament would not be able to legislate for Ireland. He can not mean that it will not be able to do so for imperial purposes, because that power is expressly reserved by the Bill. But, he asks, can it legislate for other purposes? He says: "Perhaps it can, as a matter of abstract right." But what difference is there between an abstract right and any other kind of right? None whatever. There is, indeed, a difference between forms in which right may exist. There are rights which you put in constant exercise, and there are rights which you suffer to lie dormant. We have the right in this Parliament to legislate for Ireland, and we shall continue to have it when the Bill becomes an Act. We shall retain, as a matter of pure right, the power to legislate for Ireland for all purposes whatever, for the simple reason that we can not divest ourselves of it. There is no principle more universally admitted by constitutional jurists than the absolute omnipotence of Parliament.

This omnipotence exists because there is nothing beyond Parliament or behind Parliament. We are sitting here as the nation, the whole nation; we are not delegates entrusted, like the American Congress, with specified and limited powers; we represent the whole British nation, which has committed to us the plenitude of its authority, and has provided no method of national action except through our votes. And we have, therefore, full power to legislate for every purpose. We are not checked or restrained, as is the Congress of the United States, or any other body existing under a written constitution, because the whole force and power reside in us to be exercised within these walls. The Irish members, I am sure, know perfectly that this is so. It is not a question of their asking us whether we will agree to divest ourselves of this power, because we can not do so. There is one limitation, and one only, upon our omnipotence, and that is that we can not bind our successors.

If we pass a statute purporting to extinguish our right to legislate on any given subject, or over any given district, it may be repudiated and repealed by any following Parliament—aye, even by this present Parliament on any later day.

What then, I may be asked, is the position in which we are to be placed after the concessions proposed in this Bill? It will be this: While the ultimate right to legislate will reside in, and for all English, Scottish, and imperial purposes will be exercised by, the imperial Parliament, we shall have conceded to the Irish Legislature the right to legislate on subjects upon which we do not intend to exercise the right of legislating ourselves. This is exactly what we have done with our Colonies. We have yielded to them self-governing powers; the Colonies exercise those powers; and we rarely interfere with the exercise of those powers by them. It has been pointed out in debate that in the Colonial Acts we had expressly reserved all legislative power to the imperial Parliament. But if the House had leisure to listen to a detailed argument, I could show that the reservation to which my right honorable friend seemed to refer in the Act of 1865 had a purpose and meaning different from that which he imagines. In the Act of 1867, which created the Dominion Legislature of Canada, there is no express reservation of the legislative power of the imperial Parliament, yet since then the imperial Parliament has legislated for Canada by passing Merchant Shipping Acts, a Copyright Act, and other measures which are now in force in the Dominion.

This contract, like most contracts, is a two-sided engagement. On our side it binds us not to repeal this Statute, or to alter it, or to do anything inconsistent with it, so as to prejudice the position of Ireland without summoning the Irish members; and, on the other hand, it binds the Irish Parliament, on its part, to observe in good faith the Statute in spirit as well as in letter, to act fairly under it, not to abuse or pervert the powers which it gives. While Ireland, through her Parliament, observes this contract, we shall be bound to observe our part of it; and so long as Ireland is faithful to the intentions of the Act on her side, so long will it be our duty, if we desire to modify the Act, to summon the Irish members here. But if the Irish Parliament should transgress the spirit and meaning of the Act, we, on our side, shall be released from our obligation; and then that which is in any case a legal right on our side would become also a moral right, because a breach of the contract on their side would entitle us to use our full legal rights. Now, the imposition of such a moral obligation as this is not a change which will alter the general character of the Constitution. It will leave the sovereignty of Parliament and the consequent flexibility of the Constitution as they were before, since means are provided whereby we can repeal the Act and regain any freedom which it may be supposed we are now morally, tho not legally, parting with.

Now, in the United States, Congress can not deal with the decisions of the supreme court, because those decisions are delivered as interpretations of the written Constitution, the instrument which creates Congress, and which is the supreme law of the land everywhere. The supreme court is out of the reach of Congress, not because it is a law court, but because it is the authorized interpreter, or, as one may say, the living voice of a document superior in authority to the will of Congress. But in this country Parliament is above the privy council, because we have no written Constitution, and all the courts are bound to obey the will of Parliament. Therefore, we shall not tie our hands, as the hands of Congress are tied. Under this Act Parliament will still be above the House of Lords, above the privy council, above all the courts of law anywhere within the queen's dominions. No conflict can therefore arise between the decisions of the English and the Irish judges. There can be no conflict, because the Bill provides that in every case there shall be an appeal to a final court of appeal, and the decision of that court will govern the action of every subordinate court, whether Irish or English. In cases where the construction of this Act is in question the appeal lies to the privy council; in ordinary cases it lies to the House of Lords; but in any case it will be final; therefore there can by no possibility be two sets of courts—one set in Ireland and another in England—continuing to give contradictory decisions. I admit that the system under this Bill is complicated. It can not be otherwise, for the complication is in the facts with which we have to deal.

But, sir, there is another class of instances—what I may call the negative influences—furnished us by modern Europe where nations have had this problem presented to them, and where they have shrunk from grappling fairly with it. When confronted by disaffection due to unsatisfied national sentiment, they have refused to recognize and give legitimate scope to that sentiment. What has been the consequence? Do honorable members recollect that for some years before 1830 there was a constant struggle going on between Holland and Belgium? The Belgians demanded some recognition of their nationality, some separate institutions for Belgium; but the Dutch, in their national pride, refused. In 1830 the Parisian Revolution fanned the embers into flame. The Belgians rose; Holland remained obstinate; and at last, because she had refused moderate concessions, she lost Belgium altogether. The same is the moral of the relations between Denmark and the Duchies of Schleswig and Holstein. During many years the German population of these Duchies continued to plead for a due recognition of their difference from the rest of the Danish monarchy; but the Danes said: "No, we are and will be one nation; we will not make in your favor those exceptions and special arrangements which you desire. You are Danish subjects; Danes you shall be." The Danish language was to be taught in all the schools of Schleswig, and every means was to be taken of replacing German by Danish sentiment. What was the consequence? The discontent of Schleswig and Holstein found sympathy in Germany, and the Germanic Powers intervened.

You will say that there is no great Power to interfere between us and Ireland. That is quite true. It is not always in the same way that these problems are solved. But they find their solution nevertheless, and it is a solution which usually punishes the pride and obstinacy of a dominant race. Schleswig and Holstein kept up their discontent so long, that at last the hour arrived for which they had been waiting, and Denmark saw herself deprived of those Provinces which a policy of moderate conciliation would have enabled her to retain. We have also the case of Russia in her dealings with Poland and Finland. Russia allowed Finland autonomy; and it is at this day a peaceable, prosperous, and contented Province of the Czar's dominions, inspiring him with no fear of conspiracies or revolts, altho the frontier of Finland comes almost to the gates of St. Petersburg. Russia refused to deal in the same spirit with Poland, and what were the consequences? She has, indeed, or she seems to have, crushed Poland; but I ask honorable members whether they desire to see this country imitate the methods by which Poland has been crushed? This force of nationality is a great force in human affairs. The honorable and learned member for Plymouth [Mr. Edward Clarke] spoke on Thursday night with some contempt of the feeling of nationality. I do not say that it is always a good thing. It is one of those sentiments which, tho primarily and usually good, because it binds men together by common devotion to a fine idea, may also become a destroying power and the instrument of evil. It works for good or ill, just as you choose to treat it. But it is a force which governments ignore at their peril.

We are accused of putting forward this Bill as a counsel of despair. Sir, I do not support it as a counsel of despair; I do not support it as the only alternative to a long course of coercion, altho I believe such coercion to be the only alternative policy; but I support it because I believe it to be a good thing in itself. I believe that Ireland will be better legislated for in a legislature in Dublin by its own members, because that legislature will be in sympathy with the feelings and will understand the needs of its fellow citizens. We in this Parliament—English and Scotch members—are ignorant of the wants of the Irish people. We vote at the sound of the division bell, as the party whips tell us. That has certainly been the rule of honorable members opposite, even more than of members on this side. And what does the government do? The government is guided by its chief secretary, and the chief secretary is guided by the permanent officials at Dublin Castle, so that to talk of Ireland having any real self-government is altogether idle, because Ireland is governed in and through this House, in which Irish members are in a small, and usually also an unpopular minority.

It is idle to think of legislating satisfactorily for Ireland in a House in which the Irish members constitute a small minority out of sympathy with the majority—a House chiefly composed of members who have never been in Ireland, and have no direct personal knowledge of Irish conditions and Irish sentiment—a House whose acts and votes are checked and nullified by another and an irresponsible House, in which there is not a single representative of Irish national feeling. The thing most necessary to us in this matter at this juncture is to look facts fairly and fully in the face. I have felt this strongly in reading the powerful speeches, delivered during the Easter recess, of my right honorable friend, the member for East Edinburgh [Mr. Goschen], whom I am sorry not to see in his place. He seems to me to speak like a man who does not see—who, at any rate, does not realize—the dominant facts of the situation. Those who desire a strong, repressive government for Ireland talk as if, in order to succeed in ruling and pacifying

Ireland, England and Scotland need only to put their foot down; and we have had this very day in the newspapers a vigorous and trenchant expression of that view from the leader of the Tory party.

Now, I admit that England and Scotland can govern Ireland by repression. We in Great Britain are more than thirty millions of people. We have got the men; we have got the ships and the arms; if they wish, we have got the money, too; and if Great Britain chooses to put her foot down, she can crush Ireland under an iron heel. But let me ask the question: Is this what the British people wish to do or mean to do? If our government were a despotism, sir, or such an oligarchy as ruled before the Reform Act of 1832, I could understand my right honorable friend, the member for East Edinburgh [Mr. Goschen], or Lord Salisbury making this proposition. But what are we? We are a democracy, sir—a modern democracy. A modern democracy is fitted neither by its methods of government nor by its sentiments for a policy of that sort. A democracy would not consent to, and, if it had consented, would never persist in such a policy. A democracy has a short memory; and altho it might, in a moment of exasperation, pass severe laws, it would soon forget the occasion of those laws and repeal them.

A democracy loves equality, and it could not bear to think, as it would be apt to think, that in ruling by stern laws it was oppressing the masses of the people in the interest of a landlord class. A democracy has a tender conscience, and a dislike—perhaps too strong a dislike—of severe methods; it would be pained by the fear that it was doing injustice and sanctioning harshness. A democracy loves freedom, and it would refuse to put into the hands of a government such as the Marquis of Salisbury contemplates that suspension of the Irish representation, that subjection of Ireland to arbitrary rule, which would be necessary for his purpose. I am not arguing now whether in all this democracy may be right or wrong, or whether we have done foolishly or wisely in making our government a democracy. With such questions I am not concerned, for what I ask the House is to realize the present facts and their consequences. I say that we are a democracy, and that we must, therefore, govern on democratic principles.

I have noticed that throughout this debate honorable members have been appealing to the Civil War in America, and the conduct of the Northern States in that supreme crisis, as a reason and precedent for our keeping down Ireland. The argument, when once the facts have been duly mastered, points the other way. A part of the United States rebelled on behalf of one of the worst of causes in which men ever took up arms. The North, animated by a strong sentiment of nationality, and by a hatred of slavery, determined to put that rebellion down, and did put it down. So we, if Ireland were to secede, would determine to keep her attached to this island, and by force of arms we should succeed. But it is not in war that the chief difficulty lies—it is in governing afterwards.

What did the United States do when the Civil War came to an end? First of all, they tried the experiment of governing the Southern States by military occupation, and they found that that system broke down, because it was impossible to keep the people in subjection and the country tranquil by military force alone. Then they tried to govern it by the disfranchisement of all who took part in the war against the Union; and they handed over the government to the negroes and a number of Northern adventurers, and that system broke down. Outrages, perpetrated on the negroes or on the Northern men who had come down into the Carolinas and Tennessee, became frequent, and could not be checked by the civil authorities. The condition of things in the South during those years was a scandal to the country.

Then at last, with the strong practical sense which becomes a free people, and which especially distinguishes the people of America, they came back to their original principles. They set up the Southern States as self-governing communities on the old lines; they restored the suffrage to all citizens, declaring those who had taken part in the war to be exempt from further consequences; and then the outrages came to an end, and those disorderly Southern communities became speedily prosperous and law-abiding. The example of the United States is the strongest possible case you could have to show that a democratic system must be true to itself, and that only so can it succeed.

As to the cases of Scotland and Wales, these are cases which are not now before us. I do not believe that there exists in Scotland any widespread desire and demand for a separate legislature. If ever such a demand is made by the Scottish people with anything resembling the volume of demand now made by Ireland, it will be time enough for us to consider it; and when it is considered it will be dealt with upon its own merits. No one who knows the Scottish people can doubt that they will obtain whatever they seek. But I venture to ask honorable members below the gangway whether they have realized the effect of the decision they will give if they vote against this Bill? We are exposed here to what I may call a triple fire. Besides the fire that comes from the benches opposite, and that we receive from some of those who sit behind us —the noble Marquis and those who act with him—we have had, if not a volley, yet some dropping shots (I hope they will be nothing more than dropping shots) from below the gangway. I ask those honorable members to consider what the result will be if they join the noble Marquis and the Tory party in throwing out the Bill? We know what the Tory policy is. It is force. It is repression, prolonged and

stern repression. What did the Marquis of
Salisbury tell his followers on Saturday night?
"Remember," he said to them, "that you are
the most powerful party." Yes, sir; they are
numerically the most powerful of the parties
opposed to this Bill; and if this Bill should be
rejected, and the reins of government should
unhappily pass to them, it is their policy that
will and must prevail.

Sir, the democracy of England—the new-born
democracy of England—is prepared to do what
is right by the Irish people; and I trust that the
knowledge of its purpose and its sympathy will
enable the Irish people to await in a calm and
law-abiding spirit the fulfilment of their wishes
—wishes whose justice we have now, at last, admitted, and for which, in this House and out of
this House, on every platform in Great Britain,
we shall not cease to do battle.

BALFOUR

ON THE BENEFITS OF READING[1]

(1887)

Born in 1848; nephew of Lord Salisbury; made President of the
Local Government Board in 1885; Secretary for Scotland in 1886;
Secretary for Ireland in 1887; First Lord of the Treasury in 1891, and
again in 1895 and 1900; Prime Minister in 1902.

TRULY it is a subject for astonishment that,
instead of expanding to the utmost the employment of this pleasure-giving faculty, so many
persons should set themselves to work to limit
its exercise by all kinds of arbitrary regula-
tions.

Some persons, for example, tell us that the
acquisition of knowledge is all very well, but
that it must be useful knowledge,—meaning
usually thereby that it must enable a man to
get on in a profession, pass an examination,
shine in conversation, or obtain a reputation for
learning. But even if they mean something
higher than this—even if they mean that knowledge, to be worth anything, must subserve ultimately, if not immediately, the material or
spiritual interests of mankind—the doctrine is
one which should be energetically repudiated.

[1] From an address before St. Andrews University in Scotland in
December, 1887. By kind permission of Mr. Balfour, the London
Times, and Messrs. William Blackwood & Son.

I admit, of course, at once, that discoveries the most apparently remote from human concerns have often proved themselves of the utmost commercial or manufacturing value. But they require no such justification for their existence, nor were they striven for with any such object.

Navigation is not the final cause of astronomy, nor telegraphy of electro-dynamics, nor dyeworks of chemistry. And if it be true that the desire of knowledge for the sake of knowledge was the animating motives of the great men who first wrested her secrets from nature, why should it not also be enough for us, to whom it is not given to discover, but only to learn as best we may what has been discovered by others? Another maxim, more plausible but equally pernicious, is that superficial knowledge is worse than no knowledge at all. That "a little knowledge is a dangerous thing" is a saying which has now got currency as a proverb stamped in the mint of Pope's versification,—of Pope who, with the most imperfect knowledge of Greek, translated Homer; with the most imperfect knowledge of the Elizabethan drama, edited Shakespeare; and with the most imperfect knowledge of philosophy, wrote the "Essay on Man."

But what is this "little knowledge" which is supposed to be so dangerous? What is it "little" in relation to? If in relation to what there is to know, then all human knowledge is little. If in relation to what actually is known by somebody, then we must condemn as "dangerous" the knowledge which Archimedes possessed of mechanics, or Copernicus of astronomy; for a shilling primer and a few weeks' study will enable any student to outstrip in mere information some of the greatest teachers of the past.

No doubt that little knowledge which thinks itself to be great may possibly be a dangerous, as it certainly is a most ridiculous, thing. We have all suffered under that eminently absurd individual who, on the strength of one or two volumes, imperfectly apprehended by himself and long discredited in the estimation of every one else, is prepared to supply you on the shortest notice with a dogmatic solution of every problem suggested by this "unintelligible world"; or the political variety of the same pernicious genus whose statecraft consists in the ready application to the most complex question of national interest of some high-sounding commonplace which has done weary duty on a thousand platforms, and which even in its palmiest days was never fit for anything better than a peroration.

But in our dislike of the individual do not let us mistake the diagnosis of his disease. He suffers not from ignorance, but from stupidity. Give him learning, and you make him, not wise, but only more pretentious in his folly.

I say, then, that so far from a little knowledge being dangerous, a little knowledge is all that on most subjects any of us can hope to attain, and that as a source, not of worldly profit, but of personal pleasure, it may be of incalculable value to its possessor.

But it will naturally be asked, "How are we to select from among the infinite number of things which may be known those which it is best worth while for us to know?" We are constantly being told to concern ourselves with learning what is important, and not to waste our energies upon what is insignificant.

But what are the marks by which we shall recognize the important, and how is it to be distinguished from the insignificant? A precise and complete answer to this question which shall be true for all men can not be given. I am considering knowledge, recollect, as it ministers to enjoyment, and from this point of view each unit of information is obviously of importance in proportion as it increases the general sum of enjoyment which we obtain from knowledge. This, of course, makes it impossible to lay down precise rules which shall be an equally sure guide to all sorts and conditions of men; for in this, as in other matters, tastes must differ, and against real difference of taste there is no appeal.

There is, however, one caution which it may be worth your while to keep in view: Do not be persuaded into applying any general proposition on this subject with a foolish impartiality to every kind of knowledge. There are those who tell you that it is the broad generalities and the far-reaching principles which govern the world, which are alone worthy of your attention.

A fact which is not an illustration of a law, in the opinion of these persons, appears to lose all its value. Incidents which do not fit into some great generalization, events which are merely picturesque, details which are merely curious they dismiss as unworthy the interest of a reasoning being.

Now, even in science, this doctrine in its extreme form does not hold good. The most scientific of men have taken profound interest in the investigation of the facts from the determination of which they do not anticipate any material addition to our knowledge of the laws which regulate the universe. In these matters I need hardly say that I speak wholly without authority. But I have always been under the impression that an investigation which has cost hundreds of thousands of pounds; which has stirred on three occasions the whole scientific community throughout the civilized world; on which has been expended the utmost skill in the construction of instruments and their application to purposes of research (I refer to the attempts made to determine the distance of the sun by observations of the transit of Venus), would, even if they had been brought to a successful issue, have furnished mankind with the knowledge of no new astronomical principle.

The laws which govern the motions of the

solar system, the proportions which the various elements in that system bear to one another, have long been known. The distance of the sun itself is known within limits of error, relatively speaking, not very considerable. Were the measuring rod we apply to the heavens, based on an estimate of the sun's distance from the earth, which was wrong by (say) three per cent., it would not, to the lay mind, seem to affect very materially our view either of the distribution of the heavenly bodies or of their motions. And yet this information, this piece of celestial gossip, would seem to be that which was chiefly expected from the successful prosecution of an investigation in which whole nations have interested themselves.

But tho no one can, I think, pretend that science does not concern itself, and properly concern itself, with facts which are not in themselves, to all appearance, illustrations of law, it is undoubtedly true that for those who desire to extract the greatest pleasure from science, a knowledge, however elementary, of the leading principles of investigation and the larger laws of nature, is the acquisition most to be desired. To him who is not a specialist, a comprehension of the broad outlines of the universe as it presents itself to the scientific imagination, is the thing most worth striving to attain.

But when we turn from science to what is rather vaguely called history, the same principles of study do not, I think, altogether apply, and mainly for this reason—that while the recognition of the reign of the law is the chief among the pleasures imparted by science, our inevitable ignorance makes it the least among the pleasures imparted by history.

It is no doubt true that we are surrounded by advisers who tell us that all study of the past is barren except in so far as it enables us to determine the laws by which the evolution of human societies is governed. How far such an investigation has been up to the present time fruitful in results I will not inquire. That it will ever enable us to trace with accuracy the course which States and nations are destined to pursue in the future, or to account in detail for their history in the past, I do not believe.

We are borne along like travelers on some unexplored stream. We may know enough of the general configuration of the globe to be sure that we are making our way toward the ocean. We may know enough by experience or theory of the laws regulating the flow of liquids, to conjecture how the river will behave under the varying influences to which it may be subject. More than this we can not know. It will depend largely upon causes which, in relation to any laws which we are ever likely to discover, may properly be called accidental, whether we are destined sluggishly to drift among fever-stricken swamps, to hurry down perilous rapids, or to glide gently through fair scenes of peaceful cultivation.

But leaving on one side ambitious sociological speculations, and even those more modest but hitherto more successful investigations into the causes which have in particular cases been principally operative in producing great political changes, there are still two modes in which we can derive what I may call "spectacular" enjoyment from the study of history.

There is first the pleasure which arises from the contemplation of some great historic drama, or some broad and well-marked phase of social development. The story of the rise, greatness, and decay of a nation is like some vast epic which contains as subsidiary episodes the varied stories of the rise, greatness, and decay of creeds, of parties and of statesmen. The imagination is moved by the slow unrolling of this great picture of human mutability, as it is moved by contrasted permanence of the abiding stars. The ceaseless conflict, the strange echoes of long-forgotten controversies, the confusion of purpose, the successes which lay deep the seeds of future evils, the failures that ultimately divert the otherwise inevitable danger, the heroism which struggles to the last for a cause foredoomed to defeat, the wickedness which sides with right, and the wisdom which huzzas at the triumph of folly—fate, meanwhile, through all this turmoil and perplexity, working silently toward the predestined end—all these form together a subject the contemplation of which need surely never weary.

But there is yet another and very different species of enjoyment to be derived from the records of the past, which require a somewhat different method of study in order that it may be fully tasted. Instead of contemplating, as it were, from a distance, the larger aspects of the human drama, we may elect to move in familiar fellowship amid the scenes and actors of special periods.

We may add to the interest we derive from the contemplation of contemporary politics, a similar interest derived from a not less minute and probably more accurate knowledge of some comparatively brief passage in the political history of the past. We may extend the social circle in which we move—a circle perhaps narrowed and restricted through circumstances beyond our control—by making intimate acquaintances, perhaps even close friends, among a society long departed, but which, when we have once learnt the trick of it, it rests with us to revive.

It is this kind of historical reading which is usually branded as frivolous and useless, and persons who indulge in it often delude themselves into thinking that the real motive of their investigation into bygone scenes and ancient scandals is philosophic interest in an important historical episode, whereas in truth it is not the philosophy which glorifies the details, but the details which make tolerable the philosophy.

Consider, for example, the case of the French

Revolution. The period from the taking of the Bastile to the fall of Robespierre is about the same length as very commonly intervenes between two of our general elections. On these comparatively few months libraries have been written. The incidents of every week are matters of familiar knowledge. The character and the biography of every actor in the drama has been made the subject of minute study; and by common admission, there is no more fascinating page in the history of the world.

But the interest is not what is commonly called philosophic; it is personal. Because the Revolution is the dominant fact in modern history, therefore people suppose that the doings of this or that provincial lawyer, tossed into temporary eminence and eternal infamy by some freak of the revolutionary wave, or the atrocities committed by this or that mob, half-drunk with blood, rhetoric and alcohol, are of transcendent importance.

In truth their interest is great, but their importance is small. What we are concerned to know as students of the philosophy of history is, not the character of each turn and eddy in the great social cataract, but the manner in which the currents of the upper stream drew surely in toward the final plunge, and slowly collected themselves after the catastrophe, again to pursue, at a different level, their renewed and comparatively tranquil course.

Now, if so much of the interest of the French

Revolution depends upon our minute knowledge
of each passing incident, how much more necessary is such knowledge when we are dealing
with the quiet nooks and corners of history—
when we are seeking an introduction, let us say,
into the literary society of Johnson or the fash-
ionable society of Walpole! Society, dead or
alive, can have no charm without intimacy, and
no intimacy without interest in trifles which I
fear Mr. Harrison[1] would describe as "merely
curious."

If we would feel at our ease in any company,
if we wish to find humor in its jokes and point
in its repartees, we must know something of
the beliefs and the prejudices of its various
members—their loves and their hates, their hopes
and their fears, their maladies, their marriages,
and their flirtations. If these things are beneath our notice, we shall not be the less qualified to serve our queen and country, but need
make no attempt to extract pleasure out of one
of the most delightful departments of literature.

That there is such a thing as trifling information, I do not of course question; but the frame
of mind in which the reader is constantly weigh-
ing the exact importance to the universe at large
of each circumstance which the author presents
to his notice, is not one conducive to the true
enjoyment of a picture whose effect depends
upon a multitude of slight and seemingly in-

---

[1] Frederic Harrison, the essayist and philosophical writer, a
follower of Comte.

significant touches, which impress the mind often without remaining in the memory.

The best method of guarding against the danger of reading what is useless is to read only what is interesting—a truth which will seem a paradox to a whole class of readers, fitting objects of our commiseration, who may be often recognized by their habit of asking some adviser for a list of books, and then marking out a scheme of study in the course of which all these are to be conscientiously perused.

These unfortunate persons apparently read a book principally with the object of getting to the end of it. They reach the word *"Finis"* with the same sensation of triumph as an Indian feels who strings a fresh scalp to his girdle. They are not happy unless they mark by some definite performance each step in the weary path of self-improvement. To begin a volume and not to finish it would be to deprive themselves of this satisfaction; it would be to lose all the reward of their earlier self-denial by a lapse from virtue at the end. The skip, according to their literature code, is a form of cheating: it is a mode of obtaining credit for erudition on false pretenses; a plan by which the advantages of learning are surreptitiously obtained by those who have not won them by honest toil. But all this is quite wrong. In matters literary, works have no saving efficacy. He has only half learned the art of reading who has not added to it the even more refined accomplishments of skipping and of skimming; and the first step has hardly been taken in the direction of making literature a pleasure, until interest in the subject and not a desire to spare (so to speak) the author's feelings, or to accomplish an appointed task, is the prevailing motive of the reader.

ROSEBERY

ROBERT BURNS [1]

(1896)

Born in 1847; educated at Oxford; succeeded to the Earldom in 1868;
Under-Secretary of State in 1881; first Commissioner of Works in 1884;
Foreign Secretary in 1886 and again in 1892; Prime Minister in 1894.

IT is, it must be, a source of joy and pride
to see our champion Scotsman receive the honor
and admiration and affection of humanity; to
see as I have seen this morning the long proces-
sions bringing homage and tribute to the con-
quering dead. But these have only been signs
and symptoms of world-wide reverence and devotion. That generous and immortal soul pervades
the universe to-day. In the humming city and
in the crowd of men, in the backwoods and in the
swamp, where the sentinel paces the black frontier or the sailor smokes the evening pipe, or
where, above all, the farmer and his men pursue
their summer toil, whether under the Stars and
Stripes or under the Union Jack, the thought
and sympathy of men are directed to Robert
Burns.

I have sometimes asked myself, if a roll-call
of fame were read over at the beginning of every

[1] From an address in the St. Andrew's Hall, Glasgow, on July 21,
1896, on the occasion of the Burns Centenary celebration.

century, how many men of eminence would answer a second time to their names. But of our poet there is no doubt or question. The *adsum* of Burns rings out clear and unchallenged. There are few before him on the list, and we can not now conceive a list without him. He towers high, and yet he lived in an age when the average was sublime. It sometimes seems to me as if the whole eighteenth century was a constant preparation for a constant working up to the great drama of the Revolution which closed it. The scenery is all complete when the time arrives—the dark volcanic country, the hungry, desperate people, the firefly nobles, the concentrated splendor of the court; in the midst, in her place as heroine, the dazzling queen; and during lone previous years brooding nature has been producing not merely the immediate actors, but figures worthy of the scene. What a glittering procession it is! We can only mark some of the principal figures. Burke leads the way by seniority; then come Fox, and Goethe, Nelson and Mozart, Schiller, Pitt and Burns, Wellington and Napoleon, and among these Titans Burns is a conspicuous figure—a figure which appeals most of all to the imagination and affection of mankind. Napoleon looms larger to the imagination, but on the affection he has no hold. It is in the combination of the two powers that Burns is supreme.

The clue to Burns' extraordinary hold on mankind is possibly a complicated one. It has, perhaps, many developments. If so, we have no time to consider it to-night; but I personally believe the causes are, like most great causes, simple, tho it might take long to point out all the ways in which they operate. The secret, as it seems to me, lies in two words—inspiration and sympathy.

There are two great forces which seem sheer inspiration and nothing else—I mean Shakespeare and Burns. This is not the place or the time to speak of the miracle called Shakespeare, but one must say a word of the miracle called Burns.

Try and reconstruct Burns as he was—a peasant born in a cottage that no sanitary inspector in these days would tolerate for a moment; struggling with desperate effort against pauperism, almost in vain; snatching at scraps of learning in the intervals of toil, as it were, with his teeth; a heavy, silent lad, proud of his plow. All of a sudden, without preface or warning, he breaks out into exquisite song like a nightingale from the brushwood, and continues singing as sweetly, in nightingale pauses, till he dies. The nightingale sings because he can not help it; he can only sing exquisitely, because he knows no other. So it was with Burns. What is this but inspiration? One can no more measure or reason about it than measure or reason about Niagara; and remember, the poetry is only a fragment of Burns. Amazing as it may seem, all contemporary testimony is unanimous that the man was far more wonderful than his works.

If his talents were universal, his sympathy was not less so. His tenderness was no mere selfish tenderness for his own family, for he loved all mankind, except the cruel and base—nay, we may go further and say that he placed all creation, especially the suffering and depressed part of it, under his protection. The oppressor in every shape, even in the comparatively innocent embodiment of the factor and the sportsman, he regarded with direct and personal hostility. But, above all, he saw the charm of the home. He recognized it as the basis of all society. He honored it in its humblest form, for he knew, as few know, how sincerely the family in the cottage is welded by mutual love and esteem.

His verses, then, go straight to the heart of every home; they appeal to every father and mother; but that is only the beginning, perhaps the foundation, of his sympathy. There is something for everybody in Burns. He has a heart even for vermin; he has pity even for the arch-enemy of mankind. And his universality makes his poems a treasure-house in which all may find what they want. Every wayfarer in the journey of life may pluck strength and courage from it as he pauses. The sore, the weary, the wounded will all find something to heal and soothe. For this great master is the universal Samaritan. Where the priest and the

Levite may have passed by in vain this eternal
heart will still afford resource.

There is an eternal controversy which it appears
no didactic oil will ever assuage as to Burns'
private life and morality. Some maintain that
these have nothing to do with his poems; some
maintain that his life must be read in his works;
and again some think that his life damns his
poems, while others aver that his poems can not
be fully appreciated without his life. Another
school think that his vices have been exaggerated,
while their opponents scarcely think such
exaggeration possible. It is impossible to avoid
taking a side. I walk on the ashes, knowing fire
beneath and unable to avoid them, for the topic
is inevitable. I must confess myself, then, one
of those who think that the life of Burns doubles
the interest of his poems, and I doubt whether
the failings of his life have been much exaggerated,
for contemporary testimony on that point
is strong—tho a high and excellent authority, Mr.
Wallace, has recently taken the other side with
much power and point. But the life of Burns,
which I love to read with his poems, does not
consist in his vices. They lie outside it. It is
a life of work and truth and tenderness, and
tho like all lives it has its light and shade, remember
that we know all the worst as well as
the best.

His was a soul bathed in crystal. He hurried
to avow everything. There was no reticence in
him. The only obscure passage in his life is the

love-passage with Highland Mary, and as to that he was silent not from shame, but because it was a sealed and sacred episode. "What a flattering idea," he once wrote, "is a world to come. There shall I with speechless agony or rapture recognize my lost, my ever dear Mary, whose bosom was fraught with truth, honor, constancy and love." But he had, as the French say, the defects of his qualities. His imagination was a supreme and celestial gift, but his imagination often led him wrong and never more than with woman. The chivalry that made Don Quixote see the heroic in all the common events of life made Burns (as his brother tells us) see a goddess in every girl he approached; hence many love affairs, and some guilty ones, but even these must be judged with reference to time and circumstances. This much is certain: had he been devoid of genius they would not have attracted attention. It is Burns' pedestal that affords a target. And why, one may ask, is not the same treatment measured out to Burns as to others? The illegitimate children of great captains and statesmen and princes are treated as historical and ornamental incidents. They strut the scene of Shakespeare and ruffle it with the best. It is for the illegitimate children of Burns, tho he and his wife cherished them as if born in wedlock, that the vails of wrath are reserved. There were two brilliant figures both descended from the Stuarts who were alive during Burns' life. We occupy ourselves endlessly and severely with the offenses of Burns; we heave an elegant sigh over the hundred lapses of Charles James Fox and Charles Edward Stuart.

Again, it is quite clear that, tho exceptionally sober in his earlier years, he drank too much in later life; but this, it must be remembered, was but an occasional condescendence to the vice and habit of the age. The gentry who pressed him to their houses and who were all convivial have much to answer for. His admirers, who thronged to see him, and who could only conveniently sit with him in a tavern, are also responsible for this habit so perilously attractive to men of genius, from the decorous Addison and the brilliant Bolingbroke onward. The eighteenth century records hard drinking as the common incident of intellectual eminence. To a man, who had shone supreme in the most glowing society, and who was now an exciseman in a country town, with a home which can not have been very exhilarating, with the nervous system highly strung, the temptation of the warm tavern and the admiring circle there may well have been almost irresistible.

Some attempt to say that his intemperance was exaggerated. I neither affirm nor deny it. If he succumbed it was to good-fellowship and cheer. Remember, I do not seek to palliate or excuse, and, indeed, none will be turned to dis-

sipation by Burns' example—he paid too dearly
for it. But I will say this: that it all seems infinitely little, infinitely remote. Why do we
strain at this distance to discern this dim spot
on the poet's mantle? Shakespeare and Ben
Jonson took their cool tankard at the "Mermaid." We can not afford, in the strictest view
of dietary responsibility, to quarrel with them
for it. When we consider Pitt and Goethe we
do not concentrate our vision on Pitt's bottles
of port or Goethe's bottles of Moselle. Then
why, we ask, is there such a chasm between the
"Mermaid" and the "Globe"; and why are the
vintages of Wimbledon and Weimar so much
more innocent than the simple punch-bowl of
Inverary marble and its contents?

I should like to go a step further and affirm
that we have something to be grateful for even
in the weaknesses of men like Burns. Mankind
is helped in its progress almost as much by the
study of imperfection as by the contemplation
of perfection. Had we nothing before us in our
futile and halting lives but saints and the ideal,
we might well fail altogether. We grope blindly
along the catacombs of the world, we climb the
dark ladder of life, we feel our way to futurity,
but we can scarcely see an inch around or before
us. We stumble and falter and fall, our hands
and knees are bruised and sore, and we look up
for light and guidance. Could we see nothing
but distant, unapproachable impeccability we
might well sink prostrate in the hopelessness of

emulation, and the weariness of despair. Is it not then, when all seems blank and lightless, when strength and courage flag, and when perfection seems remote as a star, is it not then that imperfection helps us? When we see that the greatest and choicest images of God have had their weaknesses like ours, their temptations, their hour of darkness, their bloody sweat, are we not encouraged by their lapses and catastrophes to find energy for one more effort, one more struggle? Where they failed, we feel it a less dishonor to fail; their errors and sorrows make, as it were, an easier ascent from infinite imperfection to infinite perfection.

Man, after all, is not ripened by virtue alone. Were it so, this world were a paradise of angels. No. Like the growth of the earth, he is the fruit of all seasons, the accident of a thousand accidents, a living mystery moving through the seen to the unseen; he is sown in dishonor; he is matured under all the varieties of heat and cold, in mists and wrath, in snow and vapors, in the melancholy of autumn, in the torpor of winter as well as in the rapture and fragrance of summer, or the balmy affluence of spring, its breath, its sunshine; at the end he is reaped, the product not of one climate but of all, not of good alone but of sorrow, perhaps mellowed and ripened, perhaps stricken and withered and sour. How, then, shall we judge anyone? How, at any rate, shall we judge a giant, great in gifts and great in temptation; great in strength, and great in weakness? Let us glory in his strength and be comforted in his weakness; and when we thank heaven for the inestimable gift of Burns, we do not need to remember wherein he was imperfect: we **can not** bring ourselves to regret that he was **made** of the same clay as ourselves.

CHAMBERLAIN

THE TRUE CONCEPTION OF EMPIRE [1]
(1897)

Born in 1836; elected Mayor of Birmingham in 1873; elected to
Parliament in 1876; President of the Board of Trade in 1880; President of the Local Government Board in 1886; Colonial Secretary in
1895–1903.

It seems to me that there are three distinct
stages in our imperial history. We began to
be, and we ultimately became, a great imperial
Power in the eighteenth century, but, during
the greater part of that time, the Colonies were
regarded, not only by us, but by every European Power that possessed them, as possessions
valuable in proportion to the pecuniary advantage which they brought to the mother country,
which, under that order of ideas, was not truly
a mother at all, but appeared rather in the light
of a grasping and absentee landlord, desiring to
take from his tenants the utmost rents he could
exact. The Colonies were valued and maintained because it was thought that they would
be a source of profit—of direct profit—to the
mother country.

That was the first stage, and when we were

[1] Delivered before the Royal Colonial Institute at its annual din-
ner, in London, March 31, 1897. Printed here by kind permission of
Mr. Chamberlain and the London *Times*.

rudely awakened by the War of Independence in America from this dream that the Colonies could be held for our profit alone, the second chapter was entered upon, and the public opinion seems then to have drifted to the opposite extreme; and, because the Colonies were no longer a source of revenue, it seems to have been believed and argued by many people that their separation from us was only a matter of time, and that that separation should be desired and encouraged, lest haply they might prove an encumbrance and a source of weakness.

It was while those views were still entertained, while the Little Englanders were in their full career, that this Institute was founded to protest against doctrines so injurious to our interests and so derogatory to our honor; and I rejoice that what was then, as it were, "a voice crying in the wilderness" is now the expressed and determined will of the overwhelming majority of the British people. Partly by the efforts of this Institute and similar organizations, partly by the writings of such men as Froude and Seeley, but mainly by the instinctive good sense and patriotism of the people at large, we have now reached the third stage in our history, and the true conception of our empire. What is that conception? As regards the self-governing Colonies we no longer talk of them as dependencies. The sense of possession has given place to the sentiment of kinship.

We think and speak of them as part of ourselves, as part of the British Empire, united to us, altho they may be dispersed throughout the world, by ties of kindred, of religion, of history, and of language, and joined to us by the seas that formerly seemed to divide us.

But the British Empire is not confined to the self-governing Colonies and the United Kingdom. It includes a much greater area, a much more numerous population, in tropical climes, where no considerable European settlement is possible, and where the native population must always vastly outnumber the white inhabitants; and in these cases also the same change has come over the imperial idea. Here also the sense of possession has given place to a different sentiment—the sense of obligation. We feel now that our rule over these territories can only be justified if we can show that it adds to the happiness and prosperity of the people, and I maintain that our rule does, and has, brought security and peace and comparative prosperity to countries that never knew these blessings before.

In carrying out this work of civilization we are fulfilling what I believe to be our national mission, and we are finding scope for the exercise of those faculties and qualities which have made of us a great governing race. I do not say that our success has been perfect in every case, I do not say that all our methods have been beyond reproach; but I do say that in almost every instance in which the rule of the

queen has been established and the great *Pax
Britannica* has been enforced, there has come with
it greater security to life and property, and a
material improvement in the condition of the
bulk of the population. No doubt, in the first
instance, when these conquests have been made,
there has been bloodshed, there has been loss of
life among the native populations, loss of still
more precious lives among those who have been
sent out to bring these countries into some kind
of disciplined order, but it must be remembered
that that is the condition of the mission we have
to fulfil. There are, of course, among us—
there always are among us, I think—a very small
minority of men who are ready to be the advocates of the most detestable tyrants, provided
their skin is black—men who sympathize with
the sorrows of Prempeh[1] and Lobengula[2] and
who denounce as murderers those of their countrymen who have gone forth at the command of
the queen, and who have redeemed districts as
large as Europe from the barbarism and the
superstition in which they had been steeped for
centuries. I remember a picture by Mr. Selous[3]
of a philanthropist—an imaginary philanthro-

---

[1] Prempeh, the king of Ashanti, was overcome by an English force
at Kumassi in 1895. A British protectorate was established over his
kingdom in January, 1896.

[2] Lobengula, the king of the Matabele, in 1893 was completely
overthrown in battle by the British, who used Maxim guns.

[3] Frederic Courteney Selous, the traveler in South Africa, who
wrote several books describing his adventures in Rhodesia and
elsewhere.

pist, I will hope—sitting cosily by his fireside and
denouncing the methods by which British civilization was promoted. This philanthropist complained of the use of Maxim guns and other
instruments of warfare, and asked why we could
not proceed by more conciliatory methods, and
why the impis of Lobengula could not be brought
before a magistrate, fined five shillings, and
bound over to keep the peace.

No doubt there is humorous exaggeration in
this picture, but there is gross exaggeration in
the frame of mind against which it was directed.
You can not have omelettes without breaking
eggs; you can not destroy the practises of barbarism, of slavery, of superstition, which for
centuries have desolated the interior of Africa,
without the use of force; but if you will fairly
contrast the gain to humanity with the price
which we are bound to pay for it, I think you
may well rejoice in the result of such expeditions as those which have recently been conducted
with such signal success in Nyassaland, Ashanti,
Benin, and Nupé—expeditions which may have,
and indeed have, cost valuable lives, but as to
which we may rest assured that for one life lost
a hundred will be gained, and the cause of civilization and the prosperity of the people will in
the long run be eminently advanced. But no
doubt such a state of things, such a mission as I
have described, involves heavy responsibility. In
the wide dominions of the queen the doors of
the temple of Janus are never closed, and it is

a gigantic task that we have undertaken when we have determined to wield the scepter of empire. Great is the task, great is the responsibility, but great is the honor; and I am convinced that the conscience and the spirit of the country will rise to the height of its obligations, and that we shall have the strength to fulfil the mission which our history and our national character have imposed upon us.

In regard to the self-governing Colonies our task is much lighter. We have undertaken, it is true, to protect them with all the strength at our command against foreign aggression, altho I hope that the need for our intervention may never arise. But there remains what then will be our chief duty—that is, to give effect to that sentiment of kinship to which I have referred and which I believe is deep in the heart of every Briton. We want to promote a closer and firmer union between all members of the great British race, and in this respect we have in recent years made great progress—so great that I think sometimes some of our friends are apt to be a little hasty, and to expect even a miracle to be accomplished. I would like to ask them to remember that time and patience are essential elements in the development of all great ideas. Let us, gentlemen, keep our ideal always before us. For my own part, I believe in the practical possibility of a federation of the British race, but I know that it will come, if it does come, not by pressure, not by anything in the nature of dictation from this country, but it will come as the realization of a universal desire, as the expression of the dearest wish of our Colonial fellow subjects themselves.

That such a result would be desirable, would be in the interest of all our Colonies as well as of ourselves, I do not believe any sensible man will doubt. It seems to me that the tendency of the time is to throw all power into the hands of the greater empires, and the minor kingdoms—those which are non-progressive—seem to be destined to fall into a secondary and subordinate place. But, if Greater Britain remains united, no empire in the world can ever surpass it in area, in population, in wealth, or in the diversity of its resources.

Let us, then, have confidence in the future. I do not ask you to anticipate with Lord Macaulay the time when the New Zealander [1] will come here to gaze upon the ruins of a great dead city. There are in our present condition no visible signs of decrepitude and decay. The mother country is still vigorous and fruitful, is still able to send forth troops of stalwart sons to people and to occupy the waste spaces of the earth; but yet it may well be that some of these sister nations whose love and affection we eagerly desire may in the future equal and even surpass our greatness. A transoceanic capital may

---

[1] Macaulay's famous prophecy, in words almost identical, may be found in one of the letters of Horace Walpole.

arise across the seas, which will throw into shade
the glories of London itself; but in the years
that must intervene let it be our endeavor, let
it be our task, to keep alight the torch of imperial
patriotism, to hold fast the affection and the
confidence of our kinsmen across the seas; so
that in every vicissitude of fortune the British
Empire may present an unbroken front to all
her foes, and may carry on even to distant ages
the glorious traditions of the British flag. It
is because I believe that the Royal Colonial Institute is contributing to this result that with
all sincerity I propose the toast of the evening.

LAURIER

ON THE DEATH OF QUEEN VICTORIA [1]
(1901)

Born in 1841; Minister of Internal Revenue in Canada in 1877; Queen's Counsel in 1880; Leader of the Liberal Party in 1887; Prime Minister in 1896; Knighted in 1897.

WE have met under the shadow of a death which has caused more universal mourning than has ever been recorded in the pages of history. In these words there is no exaggeration; they are the literal truth. There is mourning in the United Kingdom, in the Colonies, and in the many islands and continents which form the great empire over which extend the sovereignty of Queen Victoria. There is mourning deep, sincere, heartfelt in the mansions of the great, and of the rich, and in the cottages of the poor and lowly; for to all her subjects, whether high or low, whether rich or poor, the queen, in her long reign had become an object of almost sacred veneration.

There is sincere and unaffected regret in all of the nations of Europe, for all the nations of Europe had learned to appreciate, to admire, and to envy the many qualities of Queen Victoria, those many public and domestic virtues which were the pride of her subjects.

[1] From a speech delivered in the Canadian Parliament on February 8, 1901.

There is genuine grief in the neighboring nation of seventy-five million inhabitants, the kinsmen of her own people, by whom at all times and under all circumstances her name was held in high reverence, and where, in the darkest days of the Civil War, when the relations of the two countries were strained almost to the point of snapping, the poet Whittier well expressed the feeling of his countrymen when he exclaimed:

> "We bowed the heart, if not the knee,
> To England's Queen, God bless her."

There is wailing and lamentation among the savage and barbarian peoples of her vast empire, in the wigwams of our own Indian tribes, in the huts of the colored races of Africa and of India, to whom she was at all times the Great Mother, the living impersonation of majesty and benevolence. Aye, and there is mourning also, genuine and unaffected, in the farmhouses of South Africa, which have been lately and still are devastated by war, for it is a fact that above the clang of arms, above the many angers engendered by the war, the name of Queen Victoria was always held in high respect, even by those who are fighting her troops, as a symbol of justice, and perhaps her kind hand was much relied upon when the supreme hour of reconciliation should come.

Undoubtedly we may find in history instances where death has caused perhaps more passionate outbursts of grief, but it is impossible to find instances where death has caused so universal, so sincere, so heartfelt an expression of sorrow. In the presence of these many evidences of grief which come not only from her own dominions, but from all parts of the globe; in the presence of so many tokens of admiration, where it is not possible to find a single discordant note; in the presence of the immeasurable void caused by the death of Queen Victoria, it is not too much to say that the grave has just closed upon one of the great characters of history.

What is greatness? We are accustomed to call great those exceptional beings upon whom heaven has bestowed some of its choicest gifts, which astonish and dazzle the world by the splendor of faculties, phenomenally developed, even when these faculties are much marred by defects and weaknesses which make them nugatory of the good.

But this is not, in my estimation at least, the highest conception of greatness. The equipoise of a well-balanced mind, the equilibrium of faculties well and evenly ordered, the luminous insight of a calm judgment, are gifts which are as rarely found in one human being as the possession of the more dazzling tho less solid qualities. And when these high qualities are found in a ruler of men, combined with purity of soul, kindness of heart, generosity of disposition, elevation of purpose, and devotion to duty, this is what seems to me to be the highest conception of greatness, greatness which will be abundantly productive of happiness and glory to the people under such a sovereign. If I mistake not, such was the character of Queen Victoria, and such were the results of her rule. It has been our privilege to live under her reign, and it must be admitted that her reign was of the grandest in history, rivaling in length and more than rivaling in glory the long reign of Louis XIV., and, more than the reign of Louis XIV., likely to project its luster into future ages.

If we cast our glance back over the sixty-four years into which was encompassed the reign of Queen Victoria, we stand astonished, however familiar we may be with the facts, at the development of civilization which has taken place during that period. We stand astonished at the advance of culture, of wealth, of legislation, of education, of literature, of the arts and sciences, of locomotion by land and by sea, and of almost every department of human activity.

The age of Queen Victoria must be held to be on a par with the most famous within the memory of man. Of course, of many facts and occurrences which have contributed to make the reign of Queen Victoria what it was, to give it the splendor which has created such an impression upon her own country, and which has shed such a luminous trail all over the world, many took place apart and away from her influence. Many events took place in relation to which the most partial panegyrists would, no doubt, have to say, that they were simply the happy circumstance of the time in which she lived. Science, for instance, might have obtained the same degree of development under another monarch.

It is also possible that literature might have flourished under another monarch, but I believe that the contention can be advanced, and advanced truly, that the literature of the Victorian age to a large extent reflected the influence of the queen. To the eternal glory of the literature of the reign of Queen Victoria be it said, that it was pure and absolutely free from the grossness which disgraced it in former ages, and which still unhappily is the shame of the literature of other countries. Happy indeed is the country whose literature is of such a character that it can be the intellectual food of the family circle; that it can be placed by the mother in the hands of her daughter with abundant assurance that while the mind is improved the heart is not polluted. Such is the literature of the Victorian age. For this blessing, in my judgment, no small credit is due to the example and influence of our departed queen. It is a fact well known in history, that in England as in other countries, the influence of the sovereign was always reflected upon the literature of the reign. In former ages, when the court was impure, the literature of the nation was impure, but in the age of Queen Victoria, where the life of the court was pure, the literature of the age was pure also. If it be true that there is a real

connection between the high moral standard of
the court of the sovereign and the literature of
the age, then I can say without hesitation that
Queen Victoria has conferred, not only upon her
own people, but upon mankind at large, a gift
for which we can never have sufficient appreciation.

Queen Victoria was the first of all sovereigns
who was absolutely impersonal—impersonal politically, I mean. Whether the question at issue
was the abolition of the Corn Laws, or the war
in the Crimea, or the extension of the suffrage,
or the disestablishment of the Irish Church, or
Home Rule in Ireland, the queen never gave
any information of what her views were upon
any of these great political issues. Her subjects
never knew what were her personal views, tho
views she had, because she was a woman of strong
intellect, and we know that she followed public
events with great eagerness. We can presume,
indeed we know, that whenever a new policy
was presented to her by her prime minister she
discussed that policy with him, and sometimes
approved or sometimes, perhaps, dissented.

But that is not all. The most remarkable
event in the reign of Queen Victoria—an event
which took place in silence and unobserved—the
most remarkable event in the reign of the late
queen was the marvelous progress in Colonial
development, development which, based upon
local autonomy, ended in colonial expansion.

What has been the cause of that marvelous

change? The cause is primarily the personality of Queen Victoria. Of course the visible and chief cause of all is the bold policy inaugurated many years ago of introducing parliamentary constitutional government, and allowing the Colonies to govern themselves.

But, sir, it is manifest that self-government could never have been truly effective in Canada had it not been that there was a wise sovereign reigning in England, who had herself given the fullest measure of constitutional government to her own people. If the people of England had not been ruled by a wise queen; if they had not themselves possessed parliamentary government in the truest sense of the term; if the British Parliament had been as it had been under former kings in open contention with the sovereign, then it is quite manifest that Canada could not have enjoyed the development of constitutional government which she enjoys to-day. It is quite manifest that if the people of England had not possessed constitutional government in the fullest degree at home, they could not have given it to the Colonies; and thus the action of the queen in giving constitutional government to England has strengthened the throne, not only in England, but in the Colonies as well.

At the close of the Civil War, when the union of the United States had been confirmed, when slavery had been abolished, when rebellion had been put down, the civilized world was shocked to hear of the foul assassination of the wise and good man who had carried his country through that ordeal. Then the good heart and sound judgment of the queen were again manifested. She sent a letter to the widow of the martyred president—not as the queen of Great Britain to the widow of the president of the United States, but she sent a letter of sympathy from a widow to a widow, herself being then in the first years of her own bereavement. That action on her part made a very deep impression upon the minds of the American people; it touched not only the heart of the widowed wife, but the heart of the widowed nation; it stirred the souls of strong men; it caused tears to course down the cheeks of veterans who had courted death during the previous four years on a thousand battlefields.

I do not say that it brought about reconciliation, but it made reconciliation possible. It was the first rift in the clouds; and to-day, in the time of England's mourning, the American people flock to their churches, pouring their blessings upon the memory of Britain's queen. I do not hope, I do not believe it possible, that the two countries which were severed in the eighteenth century, can ever be again united politically; but perhaps it is not too much to hope that the friendship thus inaugurated by the hand of the queen may continue to grow until the two nations are united again, not by legal bonds, but by ties of affection as strong, perhaps, as if sanctioned by all the majesty of the laws of the two countries; and if such an event were ever to take place, the credit of it would be due to the wise and noble woman who thus would have proved herself to be one of the greatest of statesmen simply by following the instincts of her heart.

Sir, in a life in which there is so much to be admired, perhaps the one thing most to be admired is that naturalness, that simplicity in the character of the queen which showed itself in such actions as I have just described. From the first day of her reign to the last, she conquered and kept the affections of her people, simply because under all circumstances, and on all occasions, whether important or trivial, she did the one thing that ought to be done, and did it in the way most natural and simple.

She is now no more—no more? Nay, I boldly say she lives—lives in the hearts of her subjects; lives in the pages of history. And as the ages revolve, as her pure profile stands more marked against the horizon of time, the verdict of posterity will ratify the judgment of those who were her subjects. She ennobled mankind; she exalted royalty; the world is better for her life.

Sir, the queen is no more; let us with one heart say, Long live the king!

ASQUITH

TRADE AND THE EMPIRE [1]

(1903)

Born in 1852; Secretary of State for the Home Department, 1892–95;
Ecclesiastical Commission, 1892–95; Chancellor of the Exchequer, 1906.

A LITTLE less than six months ago, the then
Colonial Secretary startled the world by the an-
nouncement that the British Empire was in danger; that its unity could only be preserved by
preferential tariffs, and preferential tariffs involving a tax upon the necessary food of the
people of the United Kingdom. These opinions
the speaker has during the present week further
developed and defended, and with them it will
be my duty in a few minutes to come to close
quarters.

*　　*　　*　　*　　*　　*　　*

It is all very well to use this vague rhetorical
language about negotiation and standing up to
the foreigner, and not taking his insults lying
down. I want to know from Mr. Chamberlain
upon what is he going to retaliate. Here we come
to the very crux, and, indeed, the very heart, of
the whole matter. You can not retaliate effect-

---

[1] From a speech at Cinderford, October 8, 1903. By kind permission of Mr. Asquith and Messrs. Methuen & Co.

ively in this country upon protected countries without imposing a tax upon food or raw material. I give you one or two figures which have been put in very striking form by Mr. Sydney Buxton. He takes Russia and the United States, the two most protected countries in the world. Suppose you want to retaliate upon Russia. Out of our total imports from Russia, amounting to 25 millions, 23 millions, or eleven-twelfths, consist of foodstuffs and raw materials; so that we can not retaliate upon Russia without at the same time injuring either our working classes or our manufacturers, or both. What is the case of the United States? Out of 127 millions of imports from the United States in 1902, 108 millions, or five-sixths, were also foodstuffs or raw materials. The moment you begin to translate these vague platform phrases into practise, you find that they can not be carried out as a policy without doing to you here in Great Britain as great, and probably more, harm than the persons against whom that policy is used.

Mr. Chamberlain says he has two objects in view. The first is to maintain and increase the prosperity of the United Kingdom, and the second is to cement the unity of the Empire. We all agree as to these two objects, to which, I will venture to add, not by way of qualification, but simply by way of supplement, that the one end must not be sought, and can not be attained, at the expense of the other. In the long run, depend upon it, you will not promote the unity of the Empire by anything that arrests or impairs the material strength of the United Kingdom. Mr. Chamberlain says, and says truly, that the Colonies ought not to be treated as an appendage to Great Britain. I agree; and neither ought Great Britain to be treated as an appendage to the Colonies. After all—we must put in a word now and again for poor little England—after all, this United Kingdom still remains the greatest asset of the British Empire, with its 42 millions of people, with its traditions of free government, with its indomitable enterprise, with its well-tried commercial and maritime prowess. Any one who strikes a blow at the root of the prosperity of the United Kingdom is doing the worst service which can be done to the Empire to which we are all proud to belong.

Mr. Chamberlain is haunted by two specters. The first is the approaching decay of British trade, and the other is the possible break-up of the British Empire. I will endeavour to illustrate my own precepts and discuss this matter without heat and by argument. Let us see if the specters are real. Let us be perfectly sure about the disease before we resort to remedies which are admittedly heroic, and may be desperate. First of all, I ask your attention to this: Mr. Chamberlain said at Glasgow the other night —and no more astounding declaration has been made by any public man within my memory— that in the United Kingdom trade has been "practically stagnant" for thirty years. That

is the basis on which he proceeds. Let me ask
my fellow countrymen to see what has been our
condition during this era of stagnant trade.
During that period the amount assessed to the
income tax has doubled; the interest upon our
foreign investments has more than doubled; the
deposits in our savings banks have multiplied
two and threefold; the bankers' cheques cleared,
taking the annual average, have risen in amount
from 5,300 millions to over 8,000 millions sterling; and last, but not least, the wages of the
working classes have risen, measured not merely
in terms of money—tho there has been a considerable rise in our money wages—but much
more measured in their real terms, in the terms
of that which money can buy. As the Board of
Trade has told us, 100s. buys as much as 140s.
twenty years ago. Talk about Germany, the
protectionist paradise! I hope you will compare,
from the material the blue books place at your
disposal, the wages, the standard of living, and
the hours of labor of the German workmen and
your own. Well, all that has been going on—this
enormous accumulation of wealth, this steady
rise in the savings of all classes of the country—
all that has been going on through a period of
"stagnant trade."

The truth is, Mr. Chamberlain entirely ignores
the whole of our home trade, as do most of the
new protectionists, and that is at the bottom of
not a few of their fallacies. It is difficult to say
exactly what the bulk of our home trade is; but

the Board of Trade have computed that as the wages paid in the export trade are something like 130 millions, and as the total wage-bill of the country is between 700 and 750 millions, the export trade does not employ more than one-fifth or one-sixth of the whole labor of the country. I say, then, my first point is, you can not judge of the industrial condition and progress of the country by looking only at its foreign trade. You are leaving out of sight by far the most important factor in making up the account. Indeed, even a slackening in your export trade may be a proof and consequence of the activity of your trade at home. It was so in certain industries in the year 1900, and the reason why in those times exports did not increase at the same ratio as before had little or nothing to do with hostile tariffs. It was because our manufacturers and those they employed were so busy meeting the demand of the home market that they had not the time, the machinery, or the appliances to satisfy the demands from abroad. That is not all. Mr. Chamberlain begins by ignoring the home trade.

If you take the foreign trade, or, to use a better expression, trade carried on oversea, it is a perfectly absurd criterion to measure its extent or profitableness by looking, as Mr. Chamberlain does, to exports alone. It would be just as reasonable to determine a man's wealth by the amount of the man's expenditure without looking to his income, as to compare the profitableness of the foreign trade of a country by looking only at the exports. Why, if you look at what Mr. Chamberlain says, as between 1872 and 1900, there has only been a paltry rise of between 20 and 30 millions in exports; but if you look at the whole foreign trade and exports and imports together, you find a very different state of things. Take the three decennial periods. From 1873 to 1882, the oversea trade averaged 662 millions; from 1883 to 1892, the average was 696 millions; from 1893 to 1902, the average was 771 millions. In other words, if you take our trade as a whole, the annual average is considerably over 100 millions in thirty years.

But that does not complete the account of the matter. If you want to look at exports alone, even then you must not confine your attention to goods that are exported; because, in order to pay for our imports, we do a great deal more than send to foreign countries our goods. We perform services for them, and, in particular, we do services in performing the carrying trade of the world. Imagine a man coming before the public with the responsibility of a great statesman and telling them that trade is in a stagnant condition, when he has not even taken the trouble to bring into account the amount that we are earning every year by our shipping throughout the length and breadth of the world! I will just give you one figure with regard to that. The Board of Trade estimate of the annual earnings of our shipping comes to 90 millions a year, a figure Mr. Chamberlain has left altogether out of the account, altho it is strictly relevant to and strictly comparable with and belongs to the same class as the exports of our goods. Now, is that a growing or a diminishing quantity? I will compare the figures of the United Kingdom under free trade with the figures of the United States under protection. In 1870, just about the time that Mr. Chamberlain has taken for his comparisons, our tonnage of oversea shipping was 5,700,000; in 1902 it was 10,000,000 tons. In other words, it has increased very nearly 100 per cent. Now, in 1870 the oversea shipping tonnage of the United States was 1,500,000; in 1902 this had fallen to 880,000 tons, or a diminution of between 40 and 50 per cent. If it is true, as Mr. Chamberlain has told us, that we are sending less manufactured goods into the United States, you must not forget that at the same time we are performing for the United States, not gratuitously—great as is our affection for the United States—not gratuitously, but for value received, the service of carrying their goods as well as ours all over the world. While their shipping has declined owing to the excessive cost of shipbuilding which protection brings about, our shipping under free trade has most continuously and most prosperously increased.

My last criticism upon this part of Mr. Chamberlain's case is this: that he has committed an absolutely unpardonable error—unpardonable in a man who has acquainted himself with the

A B C of the subject—in taking the year 1872 as the starting year for his comparisons. If you had taken 1870, two years before, or if you had taken 1876, four years after, instead of finding only a growth of 20 to 30 millions, you would have found a growth of over 80 millions in exports; and, what is still more striking, if you had taken the exports of 1900 at the prices of 1872, you would have found that they amounted to 425 millions, or an increase of 170 millions, instead of Mr. Chamberlain's 30 millions.

To sum up what I have been saying about this, I have pointed out that this allegation—that during the last thirty years British trade has been in a stagnant condition—involves at least four distinct fallacies. Let us enumerate them once more. In the first place, it entirely ignores the home trade, which is a much more important factor than the foreign trade; in the second place, it makes exports alone the criterion of the volume of our trade; in the third place, it places among exports exported goods alone, and takes no notice of the services that we render to other countries; finally, even taking exported goods as the criterion, a year is deliberately selected which is no fair test of the matter at all. Then what becomes of the case which is the foundation of Mr. Chamberlain's contention that British trade has been in a ''stagnant'' condition during the last thirty years?

Then I come to the other assumption, which is: that unless we are prepared to establish a

preferential tariff we must look for a break-up
of the Empire. That is a pure assumption that
we are asked to accept and act upon without a
shadow of proof or even a scintilla of evidence.
For my part, I believe it to be—I use very plain
language about it—I believe it to be a calumny
on the Colonies and a slur upon the Empire.
Now, it is part of Mr. Chamberlain's case under
this head that our trade with our own Colonies
is growing faster than our trade with the rest of
the world. That is a very disputable proposition; but assuming, for the purpose of the argument, that it is true, we are all agreed in wishing that process to continue. If natural causes
are already at work bringing it into operation,
so much the better. But, anxious as we are to
do all that is prudent and practicable to develop
our trade with the Colonies, we free-traders do
not believe, at least I do not believe, it is in any
way desirable that we should have what is called
a self-contained Empire between which and the
rest of the world there are none of those commercial relations which are so fruitful of peace
and amity and good will.

But quite apart from that, let me deal with
this allegation: that unless something is done—
and that something means taxing the food of
the people of this country—unless something is
done the Colonies will break away from us. No
one has a higher and keener desire than I have
to maintain and develop those friendly relations
which of late years have so happily come into

existence between the Colonies and ourselves; but let me point out that the Colonies have absolutely no grievance of any kind against us. We give them free admission through our open door into the largest and best market in the whole world. On the other hand, they have at home complete fiscal autonomy. For my part, I believe if they had not had it the Empire would not have kept together so long. They have complete fiscal autonomy, and in the exercise of that freedom the large majority of them have erected protective tariffs, not only against foreign nations, but also against the Mother Country. I do not complain of that for a moment. If you give your Colonies freedom, as you were right to do, you must allow them to exercise it in accordance with local sentiments and local opinion.

MORLEY

HIS ADDRESS AT PITTSBURG[1]

(1904)

Born in 1838; graduated from Oxford in 1859 ; became Editor of the
Fortnightly Review in 1867; of the *Pall Mall Gazette* in 1880; elected
to Parliament in 1883; Chief Secretary for Ireland in 1886 and again
in 1892 ; Secretary for India in 1906.

WHAT is so hard as a just estimate of the
events of our own time? It is only now, a century
and a half later, that we really perceive that a
writer has something to say for himself when he
calls Wolfe's exploit at Quebec the turning point
in modern history. And to-day it is hard to
imagine any rational standard that would not
make the American Revolution—an insurrection
of thirteen little colonies, with a population of
3,000,000 scattered in a distant wilderness among
savages—a mightier event in many of its aspects
than the volcanic convulsion in France. Again,
the upbuilding of your great West on this continent is reckoned by some the most important
world movement of the last hundred years. But
is it more important than the amazing, imposing,
and perhaps disquieting apparition of Japan?
One authority insists that when Russia descended
into the Far East and pushed her frontier on

[1] Delivered on Founder's Day at the Carnegie Institute, Pittsburg,
Pa., November 3, 1904. By kind permission of the New York *Times*.
Abridged.

211

the Pacific to the forty-third degree of latitude, that was one of the most far-reaching facts of modern history, tho it almost escaped the eyes of Europe—all her perceptions then monopolized by affairs in the Levant. Who can say? Many courses of the sun were needed before men could take the full historic measures of Luther, Calvin, Knox; the measure of Loyola, the Council of Trent, and all the counter-reformation. The center of gravity is forever shifting, the political axis of the world perpetually changing. But we are now far enough off to discern how stupendous a thing was done when, after two cycles of bitter war, one foreign, the other civil and intestine, Pitt and Washington, within a span of less than a score of years, planted the foundations of the American Republic.

What Forbes's stockade at Fort Pitt has grown to be you know better than I. The huge triumphs of Pittsburg in material production—iron, steel, coke, glass, and all the rest of it—can only be told in colossal figures that are almost as hard to realize in our minds as the figures of astronomical distance or geologic time. It is not quite clear that all the founders of the Commonwealth would have surveyed the wonderful scene with the same exultation as their descendants. Some of them would have denied that these great centers of industrial democracy either in the Old World or in the New always stand for progress. Jefferson said, "I view great cities as pestilential to the morals, the health, and the liberties of man. I consider the class of artificers," he went on, "as the panders of vice, and the instrument by which the liberties of a country are generally overthrown." In England they reckon 70 per cent. of our population as dwellers in towns. With you, I read that only 25 per cent. of the population live in groups so large as 4,000 persons. If Jefferson was right our outlook would be dark. Let us hope that he was wrong, and in fact toward the end of his time qualified his early view. Franklin, at any rate, would, I feel sure, have reveled in it all.

That great man—a name in the forefront among the practical intelligences of human history—once told a friend that when he dwelt upon the rapid progress that mankind was making in politics, morals, and the arts of living, and when he considered that each one improvement always begets another, he felt assured that the future progress of the race was likely to be quicker than it had ever been. He was never wearied of foretelling inventions yet to come, and he wished he could revisit the earth at the end of a century to see how mankind was getting on. With all my heart I share his wish. Of all the men who have built up great States, I do believe there is not one whose alacrity of sound sense and single-eyed beneficence of aim could be more safely trusted than Franklin to draw light from the clouds and pierce the economic and political confusions of our time. We can imagine the amazement and complacency of that

shrewd benignant mind if he could watch all the
giant marvels of your mills and furnaces, and
all the apparatus devised by the wondrous in-
ventive faculties of man; if he could have foreseen that his experiments with the kite in his
garden at Philadelphia, his tubes, his Leyden
jars would end in the electric appliances of to-
day—the largest electric plant in all the world
on the site of Fort Duquesne; if he could have
heard of 5,000,000,000 of passengers carried in
the United States by electric motor power in a
year; if he could have realized all the rest of the
magician's tale of our time.

Still more would he have been astounded and
elated could he have foreseen, beyond all ad-
vances in material production, the unbroken
strength of that political structure which he had
so grand a share in rearing. Into this very
region where we are this afternoon, swept wave
after wave of immigration; English from Virginia
flowed over the border, bringing English traits,
literature, habits of mind; Scots, or Scoto-Irish,
originally from Ulster, flowed in from Central
Pennsylvania; Catholics from Southern Ireland;
new hosts from Southern and East Central
Europe. This is not the Fourth of July. But
people of every school would agree that it is no
exuberance of rhetoric, it is only sober truth to
say that the persevering absorption and incorporation of all this ceaseless torrent of heter-
ogenous elements into one united, stable, indus-
trious, and pacific State is an achievement that

neither the Roman Empire nor the Roman Church, neither Byzantine Empire nor Russian, not Charles the Great nor Charles the Fifth nor Napoleon ever rivaled or approached.

We are usually apt to excuse the slower rate of liberal progress in our Old World by contrasting the obstructive barriers of prejudice, survival, solecism, anachronism, convention, institution, all so obstinately rooted, even when the branches seem bare and broken, in an old world, with the open and disengaged ground of the new. Yet in fact your difficulties were at least as formidable as those of the older civilizations into whose fruitful heritage you have entered. Unique was the necessity of this gigantic task of incorporation, the assimilation of people of divers faiths and race. A second difficulty was more formidable still—how to erect and work a powerful and wealthy State on such a system as to combine the centralized concert of a federal system with local independence, and to unite collective energy with the encouragement of individual freedom.

This last difficulty that you have so successfully up to now surmounted, at the present hour confronts the mother country and deeply perplexes her statesmen. Liberty and union have been called the twin ideas of America. So, too, they are the twin ideals of all responsible men in Great Britain; altho responsible men differ among themselves as to the safest path on which to travel toward the common goal, and tho the dividing ocean, in other ways so much our friend, interposes for our case of an island State, or rather for a group of island States, obstacles from which a continental State like yours is happily altogether free.

Nobody believes that no difficulties remain. Some of them are obvious. But the common-sense, the mixture of patience and determination that has conquered risks and mischiefs in the past, may be trusted with the future.

Strange and devious are the paths of history. Broad and shining channels get mysteriously silted up. How many a time what seemed a glorious high road proves no more than a mule track or mere cul-de-sac. Think of Canning's flashing boast, when he insisted on the recognition of the Spanish republics in South America —that he had called a new world into existence to redress the balance of the old. This is one of the sayings—of which sort many another might be found—that make the fortune of a rhetorician, yet stand ill the wear and tear of time and circumstance. The new world that Canning called into existence has so far turned out a scene of singular disenchantment.

Tho not without glimpses on occasion of that heroism and courage and even wisdom that are the attributes of man almost at the worst, the tale has been too much a tale of anarchy and disaster, still leaving a host of perplexities for statesmen both in America and Europe. It has left also to students of a philosophic turn of mind one of the most interesting of all the problems to be found in the whole field of social, ecclesiastical, religious, and racial movement. Why is it that we do not find in the south as we find in the north of this hemisphere a powerful federation—a great Spanish-American people stretching from the Rio Grande to Cape Horn? To answer that question would be to shed a flood of light upon many deep historic forces in the Old World, of which, after all, these movements of the New are but a prolongation and more manifest extension.

What more imposing phenomenon does history present to us than the rise of Spanish power to the pinnacle of greatness and glory in the sixteenth century? The Mohammedans, after centuries of fierce and stubborn war, driven back; the whole peninsula brought under a single rule with a single creed; enormous acquisitions from the Netherlands of Naples, Sicily, the Canaries; France humbled, England menaced, settlements made in Asia and Northern Africa—Spain in America become possessed of a vast continent and of more than one archipelago of splendid islands. Yet before a century was over the sovereign majesty of Spain underwent a huge declension, the territory under her sway was contracted, the fabulous wealth of the mines of the New World had been wasted, agriculture and industry were ruined, her commerce passed into the hands of her rivals.

Let me digress one further moment. We have

a very sensible habit in the island whence I come, when our country misses fire, to say as little as we can, and sink the thing in patriotic oblivion. It is rather startling to recall that less than a century ago England twice sent a military force to seize what is now Argentina. Pride of race and hostile creed vehemently resisting, proved too much for us. The two expeditions ended in failure, and nothing remains for the historian of to-day but to wonder what a difference it might have made to the temperate region of South America if the fortune of war had gone the other way, if the region of the Plata had become British, and a large British immigration had followed. Do not think me guilty of the heinous crime of forgetting the Monroe Doctrine. That momentous declaration was not made for a good many years after our Gen. Whitelocke was repulsed at Buenos Ayres, tho Mr. Sumner and other people have always held that it was Canning who really first started the Monroe Doctrine, when he invited the United States to join him against European intervention in South American affairs.

The day is at hand, we are told, when four-fifths of the human race will trace their pedigree to English forefathers, as four-fifths of the white people in the United States trace their pedigree to-day. By the end of this century, they say, such nations as France and Germany, assuming that they stand apart from fresh consolidations, will only be able to claim the same relative posi-

tion in the political world as Holland and
Switzerland. These musings of the moon do not
take us far. The important thing, as we all know,
is not the exact fraction of the human race that
will speak English. The important thing is that
those who speak English, whether in old lands or
new, shall strive in lofty, generous and never-
ceasing emulation with peoples of other tongues
and other stock for the political, social, and intellectual primacy among mankind. In this noble
strife for the service of our race we need never
fear that claimants for the prize will be too large
a multitude.

As an able scholar of your own has said, Jefferson was here using the old vernacular of English aspirations after a free, manly, and well-
ordered political life—a vernacular rich in stately
tradition and noble phrase, to be found in a score
of a thousand of champions in many camps—in
Buchanan, Milton, Hooker, Locke, Jeremy Tay-
lor, Roger Williams, and many another humbler
but not less strenuous pioneer and confessor of
freedom. Ah, do not fail to count up, and count
up often, what a different world it would have
been but for that island in the distant northern
sea! These were the tributary fountains, that,
as time went on, swelled into the broad confluence
of modern time. What was new in 1776 was the
transformation of thought into actual polity.

What is progress? It is best to be slow in the
complex arts of politics in their widest sense, and
not to hurry to define. If you want a platitude,

there is nothing for supplying it like a definition. Or shall we say that most definitions hang between platitude and paradox? There are said, tho I have never counted, to be 10,000 definitions of religion. There must be about as many of poetry. There can hardly be fewer of liberty, or even of happiness.

I am not bold enough to try a definition. I will not try to gauge how far the advance of moral forces has kept pace with that extension of material forces in the world of which this continent, conspicuous before all others, bears such astounding evidence. This, of course, is the question of questions, because as an illustrious English writer—to whom, by the way, I owe my friendship with your founder many long years ago—as Matthew Arnold said in America here, it is moral ideas that at bottom decide the standing or falling of states and nations. Without opening this vast discussion at large, many a sign of progress is beyond mistake. The practise of associated action—one of the master keys of progress—is a new force in a hundred fields, and with immeasurable diversity of forms. There is less acquiescence in triumphant wrong. Toleration in religion has been called the best fruit of the last four centuries, and in spite of a few bigoted survivals, even in our United Kingdom, and some savage outbreaks of hatred, half religious, half racial, on the Continent of Europe, this glorious gain of time may now be taken as secured. Perhaps of all the contributions of

America to human civilization this is greatest. The reign of force is not yet over, and at intervals it has its triumphant hours, but reason, justice, humanity fight with success their long and steady battle for a wider sway.

Of all the points of social advance, in my country at least, during the last generation none is more marked than the change in the position of women, in respect of rights of property, of education, of access to new callings. As for the improvement of material well-being, and its diffusion among those whose labor is a prime factor in its creation, we might grow sated with the jubilant monotony of its figures, if we did not take good care to remember, in the excellent words of the President of Harvard, that those gains, like the prosperous working of your institutions and the principles by which they are sustained, are in essence moral contributions, "being principles of reason, enterprise, courage, faith, and justice, over passion, selfishness, inertness, timidity, and distrust." It is the moral impulses that matter. Where they are safe, all is safe.

When this and the like is said, nobody supposes that the last word has been spoken as to the condition of the people either in America or Europe. Republicanism is not itself a panacea for economic difficulties. Of self it can neither stifle nor appease the accents of social discontent. So long as it has no root in surveyed envy, this discontent itself is a token of progress.

What, cries the skeptic, what has become of all the hopes of the time when France stood upon the top of golden hours? Do not let us fear the challenge. Much has come of them. And over the old hopes time has brought a stratum of new.

Liberalism is sometimes suspected of being cold to these new hopes, and you may often hear it said that Liberalism is already superseded by Socialism. That a change is passing over party names in Europe is plain, but you may be sure that no change in name will extinguish these principles of society which are rooted in the nature of things, and are accredited by their success. Twice America has saved Liberalism in Great Britain. The War for Independence in the eighteenth century was the defeat of usurping power no less in England than here. The War for Union in the nineteenth century gave the decisive impulse to a critical extension of suffrage, and an era of popular reform in the mother country. Any miscarriage of democracy here reacts against progress in Great Britain.

If you seek the real meaning of most modern disparagement of popular or parliamentary government, it is no more than this, that no politics will suffice of themselves to make a nation's soul. What could be more true? Who says it will? But we may depend upon it that the soul will be best kept alive in a nation where there is the highest proportion of those who, in the phrase of an old worthy of the seventeenth century, think it a part of a man's religion to see to it that his country be well governed.

Democracy, they tell us, is afflicted by mediocrity and by sterility. But has not democracy in my country, as in yours, shown before now that it well knows how to choose rulers neither mediocre nor sterile; men more than the equals in unselfishness, in rectitude, in clear sight, in force, of any absolutist statesman, that ever in times past bore the scepter? If I live a few months, or it may be even a few weeks longer, I hope to have seen something of three elections—one in Canada, one in the United Kingdom, and the other here. With us, in respect of leadership, and apart from height of social prestige, the personage corresponding to the president is, as you know, the prime minister. Our general election this time, owing to personal accident of the passing hour, may not determine quite exactly who shall be the prime minister, but it will determine the party from which the prime minister shall be taken. On normal occasions our election of a prime minister is as direct and personal as yours, and in choosing a member of Parliament people were really for a whole generation choosing whether Disraeli or Gladstone or Salisbury should be head of the government.

The one central difference between your system and ours is that the American president is in for a fixed time, whereas the British prime minister depends upon the support of the House of Commons. If he loses that; his power may not endure a twelvemonth; if on the other hand, he keeps it, he may hold office for a dozen years.

There are not many more interesting or important questions in political discussion than the question whether our cabinet government or your presidential system of government is the better. This is not the place to argue it.

Between 1868 and now—a period of thirty-six years—we have had eight ministries. This would give an average life of four and a half years. Of these eight governments five lasted over five years. Broadly speaking, then, our executive governments have lasted about the length of your fixed term. As for ministers swept away by a gust of passion, I can only recall the overthrow of Lord Palmerston in 1858 for being thought too subservient to France. For my own part, I have always thought that by its free play, its comparative fluidity, its rapid flexibility of adaptation, our cabinet system has most to say for itself.

Whether democracy will make for peace, we all have yet to see. So far democracy has done little in Europe to protect us against the turbid whirlpools of a military age. When the evils of rival states, antagonistic races, territorial claims, and all the other formulæ of international conflict are felt to be unbearable and the curse becomes too great to be any longer borne, a school of teachers will perhaps arise to pick up again the thread of the best writers and wisest rulers on the eve of the revolution. Movement in this region of human things has not all been progressive. If we survey the European courts from the end of the Seven Years' War down to the French Revolution, we note the marked growth of a distinctly international and pacific spirit. At no era in the world's history can we find so many European statesmen after peace and the good government of which peace is the best allay. That sentiment came to violent end when Napoleon arose to scourge the world.

CAMPBELL-BANNERMAN

I

ON THE POLICY OF THE LIBERAL PARTY [1]

(1905)

Born in 1836; elected to Parliament in 1868; Financial Secretary to the War Office, 1871, 1874, 1880-82; Secretary to the Admiralty, 1882-84; Chief Secretary for Ireland, 1884-85; Secretary of State for War, 1886, 1892-95; Liberal Leader in the House of Commons, 1899-1905; Prime Minister, 1906.

WE are met to-night as Liberals in a position which we have not occupied for ten years. The Unionist Government has gone. It has executed what we may call a moonlight flitting. It has run away. Not in the broad day of the Session, not even in the twilight of October, but in the murky midnight of December. They have gone. They had long ago lost, as they well knew, the confidence of the country. They still boasted in a feeble and uncertain way of holding the confidence of the House of Commons; but, last of all and worst of all, they lost confidence in themselves. And they are gone. We were told—told emphatically and abundantly—that the method

---

[1] From a speech at the Albert Hall, London, December 21, 1905. By kind permission of Sir Henry Campbell-Bannerman, and the London *Times*.

of their going would be a masterpiece of tactical skill. Tactics! Tactics! Ladies and gentlemen, the country is tired of their tactics. It would have been better for them if they had had less of tactics and more of reality. But they have lived for some years on nothing but tactics, and now they have died of tactics.

Two characteristics are outstanding above all others in the late administration: first of all, their infinite cleverness, which was not always clever; and, secondly, an inexhaustible fund of self-approbation. Of this last quality they were possessed of so much that they have even now some of it left for their obituary notices, for you will observe that each of them is going about giving himself and his colleags the most marvelous testimony. They even carry self-esteem so far that they convinced themselves that they were the only people in this kingdom who could form a government, and that if any one else tried the effort, any cabinet which could be got together would be at once distasteful to the country and destitute of strength and unity. You see here in what the wonderful tactics consist. That was the design that lurked in the December resignation. And it has come to naught; for a Government has been formed amid the respect of our opponents, which I gratefully acknowledge, and amid the confidence and satisfaction of our friends. What lesson, then, are we to draw—for let us always be taught by the conduct of our enemies —what lesson are we to draw from their discomfiture? Surely it is to avoid those evil practises of boastfulness and over-cleverness which have brought them to ruin.

If one had had any doubt—and for my part I protest I never had any—as to the wisdom of our taking office, I think it would be dispelled by certain reassuring circumstances. In the first place, there has been no shudder through the chancelleries of Europe such as Mr. Balfour kindly anticipated. Sir Edward Grey tells me that the foreign ambassadors come to see him just as if nothing had happened. Again, consols, instead of tumbling down as they ought to have done, have actually risen. In the third place, Mr. Brodrick, who ought to know all about these matters, can not be laboring under any misapprehension as to the effectiveness of the military defense of the Empire, because this is what he said the other day: "The army required a judicious review of past efforts rather than fresh schemes, and he believed that a period of rest from doubts as to their prospects would be of great advantage to officers and men." The doubts of which he speaks, let me add, can only have come from the operations of himself and of his colleags. And last of all, we have the late prime minister who, his stratagem having completely succeeded and the trap being full, yet continues as confident after his resignation as he was before it that the general election will leave his friends in a woful minority.

What has been going on in quite recent days

in India? There has been an unbroken rule—a wise rule which we, assuredly, shall not be the first to violate—to keep questions of the internal administration of India outside the area of party politics. So far as questions of the day are concerned, I expect that it will not be your friend and my friend, Mr. John Morley, in whom the doings of the late government will find their most eloquent and energetic and unsparing critic. No; it will be one of the most distinguished and powerful members of their own party—I mean Lord Curzon. One of the problems arising from the system of military administration in India has raised an angry controversy in which a prime minister, a secretary of state, a viceroy, and a commander-in-chief, have taken their part, and which has been marked by a vehemence of altercation and recrimination that would be unedifying anywhere, but is more than unedifying where the stage of such a scene is the great dominion of India. Talk of imperialism! I know nothing, I can imagine nothing, less like a sense of our imperial responsibility than the spectacle of this controversy, so rashly raised, so tactlessly handled, so recklessly published. You may be sure that it will be our aim to restore that spirit of caution and vigorous common sense which has been the basis of British rule in India; and you may also be assured that we shall make ourselves party to no steps that involve any invasion of the sacred principle—for it is a principle recognized by each party throughout the realm of the king—the sacred principle of the subordination of the military to the civil authority.

Now, Mr. Chairman, I turn to the Colonies. It is surely unnecessary for us to make public protestations of our affection for the Colonies and our desire to bring them closer and closer to ourselves. I would say this: that the relations between the Colonies and the mother country have never been settled on the lines of party politics, but if it were that they had been so fixed and were to be so conducted, surely the democratic and progressive instincts and institutions of those great communities would find more affinity among us than among our opponents. But I have heard with relief and pleasure from Lord Elgin that he finds no trace of that tendency to disruption of which we were told but a few months ago. There is no sign of tension or friction; everything is smooth save the one ruffled spot—South Africa. Ladies and gentlemen, in South Africa the difficulties and complications are, as you know, great. I have no general statement to make to you, for we have not had time adequately to examine them. But one conclusion his majesty's government has arrived at, and it is this: to stop forthwith—as far as it is practicable to do it forthwith—the recruitment and embarkation of coolies in China, and their importation into South Africa; and instructions have been given to that effect.

A few weeks ago, at Portsmouth, I referred to our present relations with foreign powers, and

I especially hailed with approval and pleasure the agreement with the French government into which Lord Lansdowne wisely entered; and I expressed then the admiration and regard which my countrymen of all ranks and parties entertained for the great French nation. I am glad to say that my sentiment expressed in Opposition is more than confirmed in Office, and I wish emphatically to reaffirm my adhesion to the policy of the *entente cordiale*. Even more important than any actual amicable instrument is the real friendship developed between the two peoples; and one of the objects of our policy will be to maintain that spirit of friendship unimpaired. On the occasion to which I referred I alluded very briefly to the great trial through which Russia is now passing. All that I will say now, as I said then, is this—that we have nothing but good feelings toward that great people. In the case of Germany also I see no cause whatever of estrangement in any of the interests of either people, and we welcome the unofficial demonstrations of friendship which have lately been passing between the two countries. With other European powers our relations are most friendly. And when we pass beyond the bounds of Europe we have on the one hand Japan, our relations with which nation are sufficiently known to the world by the recent treaty; and, on the other hand, we have the United States of America, with the government and people of which country we are bound by the closest ties of race, tradition, and fellowship. Ladies and gentlemen, this is a most pleasing outlook, which I trust will not be marred by any events that can occur.

As to our general policy toward our neighbors, our general foreign policy, it will remain the same in Government as it was in Opposition. It will be opposed to aggression and to adventure; it will be animated by a desire to be on the best terms with all nationalities, and to cooperate with them in the common work of civilization. I believe, by the way, that in the execution of this policy we have a notable ally in our present fiscal system—a great guarantee of peace and a preventive against the possibility of commercial and tariff wars. We Liberals, let us not forget it, are the heirs of a great and inspiring tradition. That tradition was founded in days when public opinion was opposed to any attempt to regulate differences by an appeal to the reason and conscience of mankind. Mr. Gladstone defied the public opinion of his day. He took his stand on higher ground, and by referring the Alabama dispute to arbitration he established a precedent of priceless value to mankind. How proud and how pleased we ought to be to have among us, and in the circle of the cabinet, a veteran statesman who took part in that great undertaking, and who remains now, as he was then, one of the truest of patriots and the staunchest and soundest of politicians. I rejoice that since that time the principle of arbitration has made great strides, and that to-day it is no longer counted weakness for any of the Great Powers of the world to submit those issues which would once have been referred to the arbitrament of self-assertion and of passion, to a higher tribunal.

Ah! but, ladies and gentlemen, it is vain, it is vain, to seek peace if you do not also ensue it. I hold that the growth of armaments is a great danger to the peace of the world. A policy of huge armaments keeps alive and stimulates and feeds the belief that force is the best, if not the only, solution of international differences. It is a policy that tends to inflame old sores and to create new sores. And I submit to you that as the principle of peaceful arbitration gains ground it becomes one of the highest tasks of a statesman to adjust those armaments to the newer and happier condition of things. What nobler *rôle* could this great country assume than at the fitting moment to place itself at the head of a league of peace, through whose instrumentality, this great work could be effected?

I now pass to the question of economy and finance—a very natural transition—and I think you may look with confidence to the action that will be taken by my friend, the chancellor of the exchequer. But where are we to begin? We want two things. We want relief from the pressure of excessive taxation, and at the same time we want money to meet our own domestic needs at home, which have been too long starved and neglected owing to the demands on the taxpayer for military purposes abroad. How are

these desirable things to be secured if in the time
of peace our armaments are maintained on a war
footing? Remember that we are spending at
this moment, I think, twice as much on the army
and navy as we spent ten years ago. There may
be, and I believe there are, fresh sources of taxation to be tapped. We may derive something
from the land, something from licenses; and some
irksome inequalities of taxation may be relieved.
But even so, with an increasing military expenditure, how can we do the work of reform
that remains to be done at home and at the same
time bring relief to the taxpayers? Do not let
us mind if in their folly they call us "Little
Englanders." I at least am patriot enough not
to desire to see the weakening of my country by
such a waste of money as we have had for the
last ten years.

What has it brought us, this waste of money
for ten years? Shall I recite some links in the
dismal and ugly chain? Dear money. Lower
credit. Less enterprise in business and manufactures. A reduced home demand. Therefore,
reduced output to meet it. Therefore, reductions
in wages, increase of pauperism, non-employ-
ment. The fact is, sir, you can not pile up debt
and taxation as they have been piled up without
feeling the strain in every fiber of society. We
are going to have a good deal said for the next
few weeks about free trade. Let me add another
thing. Did you ever hear a fiscal reformer pleading for economy, or crying out for lighter taxes

and fewer of them? No, sir, if peace and retrenchment were the order of the day, Othello's occupation would be gone. Expenditure calls for taxes, and taxes are the plaything of the tariff reformer. Militarism, extravagance, protection are weeds which grow in the same field, and if you want to clear the field for honest cultivation you must root them all out. For my own part, I do not believe that we should have been confronted by the specter of Protection if it had not been for the South African War.

Well, ladies and gentlemen, so much for peace: so much for economy—two cardinal Liberal principles. And here is another—self-government and popular control. We believe in that principle, not only on the grounds of justice and on the grounds of effective administration, but on this other ground: that it exercises a wholesome influence on the character of the people who enjoy the privilege. But now this is the foundation of our educational policy: that the people of the district should control and manage the schools. It is the foundation of our licensing policy. But if I seek for illustrations, why did I not take the greatest and most conspicuous of all—a crowning instance? What other than this is the foundation of our Irish policy—that those domestic affairs which concern the Irish people only and not ourselves should, as and when opportunity offers, be placed in their hands? Down to last spring we had reason to believe that even the late government and their party had come round to see

the wisdom of such a policy. They had already
endowed the people of Ireland with the command
of county government; they had pledged £112,-
000,000 of British credit for the tenants of Ireland; and, lastly, their viceroy had been authorized to declare that Ireland was henceforth to
be governed according to Irish ideas. They have
started back from that position; but, oh! ladies
and gentlemen, give them time. They can not
escape from the logic of their own acts, and they
will return to that which is the path of justice
and wisdom, and also of safety.

When I come to the policy of constructive
social reform, I am principally conscious that I
must make a reiteration of things which I have
been saying up and down the country for the last
three or four years. But I can promise you
this: that it will always be the same story. We
desire to develop our undeveloped estates in this
country; to colonize our own country; to give
the farmer greater freedom and greater security
in the exercise of his business; to secure a home
and a career for the laborer, who is now in many
cases cut off from the soil. We wish to make the
land less of a pleasure-ground for the rich and
more of a treasure-house for the nation. Now,
why can not Mr. Chamberlain drop his project of
taxing corn and cheese and so forth, and come
back to his old love of three acres and a cow?
This question, including these great problems,
can not be neglected, because, after all, the health
and stamina of the nation are bound up with the

maintenance of a large class of the workers on the soil. The town population redundant, the country population decimated—it is a subversion of healthy national life. Now, in passing, let me mention one thing which the government have resolved to do. Few things, we think, are more capable of benefiting both the towns and the country districts than a development, if that can be given to our system, of canal communication, and promoting the use of waterways, which will facilitate transit, which will open markets, which will bring town and country together. We have, therefore, resolved to ask the king to appoint a royal commission to inquire into the whole of that question, because we believe that great benefit to the nation may come from it.

Now, I know that on the great question in regard to which we are to give our verdict in the course of a few weeks your minds are made up, and therefore I will not enter even for a moment on arguments connected with it. I rejoice to think that since the free trade controversy was first raised, there has been no sign of faltering or wavering on our side, and that Liberalism has been true to its historic mission. In the great struggle which will shortly be upon us, I do not think it too much to say that all that we Liberals hold dear is at stake, because, if once you open the door to Protection, what hope is there for those great objects of reform and economy upon which our hearts are set? Depend upon it, that in fighting for our open ports, and for the cheap food and material upon which the welfare of the people and the prosperity of our commerce depend, we are fighting against those powers, privileges, injustices, and monopolies which are unalterably opposed to the triumph of democratic principles. Be confident, therefore; but I would ask you not to be overconfident. Against you is a strong coalition of interests and powers. Against you is a wealthy and a great party, divided indeed—as we have been amused to observe and to watch its little developments— divided in the details of fiscal strategy, but united in its determination to undermine and overthrow the citadel of free trade. Let us, then, be worthy of our fathers, who went before us and won for us this great privilege of freedom; and let us beware lest, through any fault of ours, through slackness, or indifference, or overconfidence on our part, so great and vital a national interest is imperiled.

II

HIS "THE DUMA IS DEAD: LONG LIVE THE DUMA," SPEECH[1]

(1906)

THE majority of you have not come here—and I think you will wish this to be understood —as the accredited delegates of your respective parliaments. This gathering is unofficial. But you are here, if I read the times aright, in the fullest sense as the accredited representatives of your fellow countrymen and women, and in this capacity you are entitled to express, with an authority attaching to no other assembly in the world, the conscience, the reason, and the sentiments of a large and not the least influential portion of the human race. In addressing you I feel that I am not so much speaking to the representatives of diverse States of Europe and America as to the exponents of principles and hopes that are common to us all, and without which our life on earth would be a life without horizon or prospect.

With the purpose of your mission, let me say at once, his majesty's government desire un-

[1] Delivered in the French language in the Royal Gallery of the House of Lords, London, at the opening of the Interparliamentary Conference, July 23, 1906. From a copy in English kindly furnished by Sir Henry for this work.

reservedly to associate themselves. It is their hope that your deliberations will do much to promote a closer understanding between the nations.

You have indeed done much since the new century began to give shape and substance to the growing, the insistent desire that war may be banished from the earth. All of us, I suppose, can remember a time when such a gathering as this would have evoked the derision of those who call themselves practical men. You would have been called dreamers, and your plans for substituting equitable arrangement for the license and ferocity of war would have been denounced as dangerous quixotry. Gentlemen, let us be charitable in our judgment of those misguided men and those dark ages. We are all creatures of habit. And by habituating the world to the idea that peaceful arbitrament can adjust such differences as diplomacy has failed to solve, you have opened men's eyes; you have cleared their minds.

Gentlemen, it must be a cause of delight and encouragement to you to feel that a great step has been taken toward the realization of an ideal. I believe that there are now in existence at present thirty-eight arbitration agreements between the different Powers. These instruments have all been framed since October, 1903. Thanks to Lord Lansdowne, Great Britain has entered into agreements with ten Powers, by virtue of which all legal questions arising be-

result of such overwhelming sacrifices of money, of men, of ideals, and of civil dignity the sense of security has indeed been attained? Is it not evident that a process of simultaneous and progressive arming defeats its own purpose? Scare answers to scare, and force begets force, until at length it comes to be seen that we are racing one against another after a phantom security which continually vanishes as we approach. If we hold with the late Mr. Hay that war is the most futile and ferocious of human follies, what are we to say of the surpassing futility of expending the strength and substance of nations on preparations for war, possessing no finality, amenable to no alliances that statesmanship can devise, and for ever consuming the reserves on which a State must ultimately rely when the time of trial comes, if come it must—I mean the well-being and vitality of its people?

Do not imagine that I wish to discourage you by contrasting the hard facts of the situation with the aspirations which we all share. That is the last thing that I have in my mind. I am not despondent about the future.

In the first place, it is only a few short years since peace was a wanderer on the face of the earth, liable at any moment to be trampled upon and despitefully used; and if wars and preparations for wars have not ceased since she found a rest for the sole of her foot at The Hague, remember that time is needed for the growth of confidence in the new order of things, and that allowance must be made for the momentum of the past which thrusts the old régime forward upon the new.

Remember, too, that the people are on your side. I know it is said that democracy is as prone to war as any other form of government. But democracy, as we know it, is a late comer on the world's stage, where it has barely had time to become conscious of its characteristic powers, still less to exert them effectively in its external relations.

The bonds of mutual understanding and esteem are strengthening between the peoples, and the time is approaching when nothing can hold back from them the knowledge that it is they who are the victims of war and militarism; that war in its tawdry triumphs scatters the fruits of their labor, breaks down the paths of progress, and turns the fire of constructive energy into a destroying force.

In this connection I can not refrain from saying for myself, and I am sure for every one in this great and historic assembly, how glad we are to welcome among us to-day the representatives of the youngest of parliaments—the Russian Duma. We deeply appreciate the circumstances of their appearance in our midst. It is, I venture to think, of good augury for your movement and for the future of Europe that the first official act of the Russian Parliament in regard to affairs outside the Russian Empire has been to authorize its delegates to come here to

Westminster and to join hands with us in the assertion of those great principles of peace and good will which were so incalculably advanced by the head of the Russian State, the author and convener of the first Hague Congress.

I make no comment on the news which has reached us this morning; this is neither the place nor the moment for that. We have not a sufficient acquaintance with the facts to be in a position to justify or criticize.

But this at least we *can* say, we who base our confidence and our hopes on the parliamentary system: New institutions have often a disturbed, if not a stormy youth. The Duma will revive in one form or another. We can say with all sincerity, "The Duma is dead: long live the Duma."

The time is approaching to which we are all looking forward with intense interest and anxious hope when the delegates of your various nationalities find themselves once again at The Hague, there to renew their labors in the cause of peace. I can only end as I began by wishing success to your deliberations. May they pave the way to far-reaching and beneficent action.

Tell your governments when you return home —what the members of the British Parliament, whom I see before me, are never tired of telling me—that example is better than precept, that actions speak louder than words; and urge them in the name of humanity to go into The Hague Congress, as we ourselves hope to go, pledged to diminished charges in respect of armaments. Entreat them to go there with a belief in the good disposition of nations to one another, such as animates you, the members of a score of parliaments, and may it be your great reward, when you next assemble a year hence, to know that as a result of your labors the light of peace burns with a steadier and a more radiant flame.

LOREBURN

ON THE POLICY OF THE ENGLISH LIBERALS [1]

(1906)

Born in 1846; became a Barrister in 1871; a Q. C. in 1882; elected to Parliament in 1880; Solicitor-General in 1894; Attorney-General in 1894; decorated for service in the Venezuelan Boundary case; Lord Chancellor in 1906.

THE parliament which was returned in January is more remarkable for intellectual power, for sincerity of purpose, and for a fixed determination to achieve its ends, than any parliament in this country for many long years. We have been told that this House of Commons was going to have a short, if not a merry, life, and that it would be replaced soon by something very much preferable. I have no such idea. I believe that this House of Commons represents a feeling and a force in this country which has been retarded already for about twenty years. The forces held back from 1885 have now reasserted themselves, and the spirit of progress will be lasting and durable. Therefore all those who

[1] From a speech at the National Liberal Club, London, on July 11, 1906. By kind permission of Lord Loreburn and the London *Tribune*. This was originally a newspaper report of an impromptu speech printed in the third person. It has been altered here to the first person.

are disposed to be critics of the present House of Commons might well consider whether, if they turned out the 670 evil spirits there now, they might not have 670 still more evil spirits in their places.

The present parliament is, I believe, more intent upon what is called "social reform" than any other class of subjects—and quite rightly. I am not going to dwell upon those topics; I agree with the most advanced upon nearly all—in fact, upon all—those subjects, whether of land, or liquor, or housing reform. We all know perfectly well what are the necessities of our country, and where the shoe pinches. But I wish to suggest to those who hold reforming views that they must not confine themselves simply to one of those questions, or even to all of those questions put together.

They must remember that this country is part of a very great empire, with dangerous foreign relations, and unless we can come to a sound view with regard to what is called Imperialism, and in regard to foreign relations, we shall have to whistle for social reform.

For that reason I am glad so much attention has of late been concentrated upon his majesty's dominions across the sea. I do not in the least agree with the point of view which has been so pushed by the late government, and which I believed has resulted in immense trouble and immense loss. But it is most important for us to see clearly, and to make up our minds in regard to those questions for ourselves. We are charged with being indifferent to the British Empire. Some other critics, and particularly Mr. Chamberlain, appear to take pleasure in showing how unjust and how unfriendly Liberals are to their colonial fellow countrymen. Nothing of the kind.

I desire, and believe we all desire, unfeignedly and without reserve, to maintain in their present happy relations the ties that subsisted between us and our colonial kindred. We heartily wish and mean that those relations shall subsist for ever, and we are not content to contemplate any other future. But we think it not wise to forbear from facing facts. We have to look at things as they are, and not as we wish them to be.

There are certain things we ought to remember in connection with them. One is that since the end of the Napoleonic wars ninety years ago, almost all the wars and expeditions this country has engaged in, have been due either to India or to the other colonies and dependencies of the crown. Almost with one exception, save for the Indian wars, the cost of all those wars has fallen almost exclusively upon the people of the United Kingdom.

They were small countries and young countries, and required the protection of the mother country. But it is a fact that ought to be remembered that our dangers of collision with other countries arose by reason of their colonial possessions. We have to bear in mind that whereas we were fortunately living in an island, in our dependencies and colonies we are coterminous with every great Power in the world —with the United States in America, with Germany, France, Italy, Russia, China, Persia, and Turkey elsewhere, and practically with Japan, where a short interval of sea does not really separate us.

About a hundred and fifty years ago, at the commencement of the Seven Years' War, when Washington, then a major serving his majesty, King George II., encountered a force of French and Redskins in Virginia, and fired upon them, it was said that a shot fired in the backwoods of Virginia had set all Europe in a blaze. So it was in Britain now. By reason of the immensity of her frontier and the contiguity of every great power in the world, a rash thing done here, a hasty thing done elsewhere, might bring about a conflagration. "Always be generous to the man on the spot!" Yes; but let them not allow a proconsul to shape the policy of this country.

There is another point: By reason of those vast possessions—of which it is idle and foolish to boast, but the full responsibility of which we ought to feel—we are always confronted with the native question. And I venture to think that in the near future the native question will be a more serious one even than it has been in the past.

What does it mean? To understand it requires

an effort of the imagination which people accustomed to the long traditions of civilization
can hardly realize. It means that people who
are in a state of complete savagery and barbarism, plunged in ignorance and superstition,
backward in physical and every other development, are suddenly confronted with the blaze
of an ancient civilization in its most hostile and
most dangerous form. They were required at
once to submit, and expected instantly to appreciate the advantages to themselves arising
from their submission. One could not so suddenly quell the primal passions and instincts of
mankind.

I should like to give an illustration. About
seven years ago I was concerned, as one of the
counsel for Great Britain, before the international tribunal which decided the Venezuelan
boundary, and I recall perfectly one thing which
made a deep impression upon my mind, and
which gave me more pride in the British flag—
a silent pride, I hope—than could be derived
from some of the more uproarious meetings. The
point was: What, at a particular place, was the
boundary-line between Great Britain and another country? Proof was given of a tradition
handed down from father to son among a people
so perfectly savage that their whereabouts, their
very dwelling, was unknown—a nomad, wander-
ing people of the woods. This was the tradition: ''The line where the British territory begins is along this river.'' And when the ques-

tion was asked why it was remembered, the reply was that father had told son, from generation to generation, "If you pass that river you are safe."

We must also look to foreign relations. We are called cosmopolitan by our critics, the friends of every country but our own. That is not so. We are the friends of our own country first and foremost—but there is no nationalism worth having which does not cast its eye beyond the border of its own nationality. We wish our country to be friendly with other countries in the interest of our own. Why should we not be friendly? I am not aware of any cause which separates us in enmity from any country in the world. I know many reasons why we should cultivate their friendship.

Swift, in one of his memorable pieces, was pleading against the abolition of Christianity. After giving a variety of reasons, he ended by saying that, if Christianity were abolished the Funds would fall at least a quarter per cent. Swift reserved that argument to the last, on the ground that his intelligent hearers would probably consider it to be the best and most cogent. I will offer you a fiscal reason to show what quarreling means. Between 1898 and 1905 British consols had fallen about 20 per cent. and Russians about 30 per cent. Germany, which had been much more moderate in that way, had fallen about 10 per cent., but the funds of Spain and Italy, which had both rather forsworn militarism, had each risen 15 per cent. I present that as an argument in the spirit of Dean Swift.

There are hopeful signs for the future. In the first place, our brethren in the Colonies are undoubtedly relying more and more on their own resources. Canada had taken over the garrison. Natal is conducting at her own expense a war which I greatly deplore, and which I hope will soon be ended. I have no doubt that our colonial brethren are just and will act justly and fairly toward them.

In the last few years there have been increased proofs of international cooperation. We all recollect the noble efforts of President Roosevelt to end the Russo-Japanese War and the signal success with which they were attended. We recall the European Conference at Algeciras, where a difficult and perhaps dangerous question was solved by agreement in a spirit which could not have been looked for twenty years ago. We have established most friendly relations with the United States and also with France. I do not know why we should stop with France and the United States, and why we should not also go forward to Russia and to Germany. Lastly, we have The Hague Conference. There was one seven years ago, and there will soon be another held. I am sure you all hope that it may lead to an increased recourse to arbitration and a diminution in the armaments of nations.

The factor which should interest us most, and over which we have the best means of control, is the spirit and temper of our own people. I believe that has undergone a great change for the better, reverting to the time-honored policy of this country; and I trust that, however keen in the work of social reform the new Parliament may be, it will never lose sight of these colonial and foreign questions; but we must remember that it will have to make a choice. If you will have a warlike and aggressive policy, you can not by any possibility have effective social reform.

END OF VOL. V